Joomla! 1.5x Customization

Make Your Site Adapt to Your Needs

Create and customize a professional Joomla! site that
suits your business requirements

Daniel Chapman

PUBLISHING

BIRMINGHAM - MUMBAI

Joomla! 1.5x Customization
Make Your Site Adapt to Your Needs

First published: August 2009

Production Reference: 1180809

Published by Packt Publishing Ltd.
32 Lincoln Road
Olton
Birmingham, B27 6PA, UK.

ISBN 978-1-847195-16-6

www.packtpub.com

Cover Image by Vinayak Chittar (vinayak.chittar@gmail.com)

Credits

Author
Daniel Chapman

Reviewers
Lesley A. Harrison
Oland T. Whitecotton, III
Tom Canavan

Acquisition Editor
Douglas Paterson

Development Editor
Dilip Venkatesh

Technical Editor
Bhupali Khule

Indexer
Monica Ajmera

Editorial Team Leader
Akshara Aware

Project Team Leader
Lata Basantani

Project Coordinator
Rajashree Hamine

Proofreader
Jeff Orloff

Drawing Coordinator
Nilesh Mohite

Production Coordinator
Aparna Bhagat

Cover Work
Aparna Bhagat

About the Author

Daniel Chapman started his career as an Oracle database consultant and trainer, working for various Australian universities, telecommunication companies, and also Oracle Australia. This work helped him develop a keen sense of the value of development standards and analysis processes.

After ten years in the Oracle arena, he wanted a change of pace, so he moved to Japan and started working in web development in 2004. He quickly picked up PHP, JavaScript, HTML, and CSS while experimenting with various CMSes.

Finally deciding on Joomla! as his CMS of choice, Daniel initially began working as a consultant, developing sites and producing a few small extensions before starting one of the first Open Source Extension Clubs: NinJoomla (`http://www.ninjoomla.com`). Eventually, he changed the club's name to Ninja Forge (`http://ninjaforge.com`), and both he and the club have since become quite well known in the Joomla! sphere.

While this is Daniel's first book as an author, he has been a technical reviewer on several books including *Choosing an Open Source CMS* (Packt Publishing) and *Joomla! 1.5 Extension Development* (Packt Publishing).

I would like to thank my wife, Kyoko, for her seemingly endless support of my work, even when it takes time away from us being together. I can't thank her enough for being there for me.

Also I would like to thank my parents for always believing in me, even when no one else would, giving me the confidence to keep going when otherwise I might have given up.

About the Reviewers

Lesley A. Harrison has more than ten years experience working in the world of IT, having served as a Systems Administrator for a multinational IT outsourcing company, and later a database administrator for a British utility company. Today, Lesley runs her own video gaming site, Myth-Games.com, and works as a freelance web developer. She has clients all over the world, running a range of Joomla!, WordPress, and other open source CMSes, as well as some custom-coded solutions.

Lesley is currently working on the *Beginner's Guide to WordPress-MU*, which will be published by Packt Publishing in December 2009.

> I would like to thank my husband, Mark, for keeping the flow of coffee coming, and Moose, for many hours of fun.

Oland T. Whitecotton, III is a certified PHP and MySQL developer with over 8 years of experience. He has worked for the largest debt consolidation company in America, Credit Solutions, as well as media publisher Idearc (think Superpages.com) and the employment web site Monster.com.

Tom Canavan has been in the computer and IT industry for 24 years and is currently working as the Chief Information Officer for a new Internet Security Startup.

He is author of the Packt Publications book, *Joomla! Web Security* and the book *Dodging the Bullets - a disaster preparation Guide for Joomla! Websites*.

Table of Contents

Preface

Setting up a basic Joomla! web site is a relatively simple process, and there have been many articles and books outlining the process. However, the next step proves difficult, and often expensive for most people, but it is the most important one. That is customizing the site to bring their vision fully to life. Understanding how and why to make these customizations, is essential to having a successful, professional site, but there has been very little written about how to take this step.

This book will help you to take your web site to this next step, guiding you through how to customize different parts and aspects of your site, allowing you to separate your site from the crowd of other Joomla! sites without having to pay an arm and a leg hiring developers to do it for you. It will also show you how to turn your site into a profitable business via these customizations.

You will be taken beyond the basics of Joomla!, and given an insight into the techniques and tools used by the professionals to rapidly develop unique, custom sites. This will enable you to develop your own professional-quality Joomla! site without assistance, saving you time and money. You will learn how modules, plugins, components, and templates are constructed, and how to make changes to them, giving you the confidence to make more elaborate changes to your site. On top of this will be a look at common problems Joomla! site developers face and how best to deal with them.

You will also learn techniques for building a business with Joomla!, as we step through building a subscription-based web business. Then we will look at marketing and monetizing this business fully to maximize our return.

What this book covers

Chapter 1 The Skills Required to Customize Joomla! – You will be given a clear understanding of why Joomla! came to be and how it fits into the Internet ecosystem, and how the technologies of HTML, CSS, JavaScript, PHP, and MySQL fit together to help you produce your site.

Chapter 2 Setting Up Our Environment – Here, you will be introduced some of the tools and the environment used by professionals to ensure that their work is done as swiftly as possible while still maintaining top quality.

Chapter 3 Planning Our Site – Before we get into the actual building of the site, we will cover how to plan your site properly and why this is essential to a successful site. You will also be shown how to choose the best extensions for building your desired site.

Chapter 4 Installing and Configuring Extensions – Here, you will see how to clean out a new Joomla! installation of unneeded content and extensions, then how to install and configure most of your extensions. We will also begin work on our example site.

Chapter 5 Installing and Modifying Templates – Here we will show you how to find, choose, and then customize a template to match the needs of your site, making changes to the HTML, CSS, PHP, and images.

Chapter 6 Customizing Modules – After templates we will look at how to customize the functionality and appearance of modules so that they can do what we need. You will be shown how a Joomla! module is designed and built.

Chapter 7 Customizing Plugins – In a similar style to Chapter 6, we will look at how plugins operate within Joomla, and then at how to modify the output of a content plugin.

Chapter 8 Customizing Components – The most difficult of extensions to modify, components, are made clear in this chapter. You will understand how to identify the differences between traditional style and modern style Joomla! components and then make changes to one to better suit our site.

Chapter 9 Finding and Fixing Problems – Here we will look a some of the common problems Joomla! web site developers face, and the ways we can solve them.

Chapter 10 Promoting and Tracking – In this chapter you will learn different methods for promoting and marketing your web site successfully, and how to track that success.

Chapter 11 Monetizing Our Site – The final chapter will go over some different methods for monetizing your site, extending what we have done in our sample site.

What you need for this book

You will need a correctly installed Joomla! 1.5 web site, and a working Internet connection.

Who this book is for

This book is written for people with basic knowledge of Joomla!, who want to expand their skills and move from simply assembling extensions, and installing a template to truly customizing their own site.

Readers are expected to have functional knowledge of Joomla! and a very basic understanding of terms such as FTP, PHP, HTML, CSS, and JavaScript, even if they have no real knowledge of the workings behind these terms. This book does not cover topics such as installing Joomla! and extensions, or creating content.

The ideal reader is one who wishes to build a successful business web site using Joomla! and is interested in making as well as saving money by applying professional tools and techniques to the development, monetization, and marketing of their site. Non-business focused site owners can still benefit greatly from the book, however, if they wish to add a level of professionalism to their work.

Conventions

In this book, you will find a number of styles of text that distinguish between different kinds of information. Here are some examples of these styles, and an explanation of their meaning.

Code words in text are shown as follows: "We take the $article parameter which was passed in, and we are going to assign a new value to its text attribute."

A block of code will be set as follows:

```
class plgContentNJaccess extends JPlugin {

    function plgContentNJaccess ( &$subject ) {
            parent::__construct( $subject );
            $this->_plugin = JPluginHelper::getPlugin('Content',
                                            'ninjaaccess');
            $this->_params = new JParameter($this->_plugin->params);
    }
```

When we wish to draw your attention to a particular part of a code block, the relevant lines or items will be shown in bold:

```
<files>
<filename module="mod_fbmodule">mod_fbmodule.php</filename>
 <filename>index.html</filename>
               <filename>helper.php</filename>
<folder>tmpl</folder>
</files>
```

New terms and **important words** are shown in bold. Words that you see on the screen, in menus or dialog boxes for example, appear in our text like this: "Next, click on **Extensions | Module Manager** and find our module."

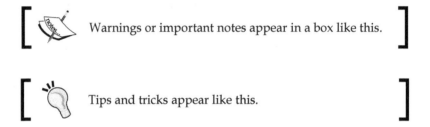

Warnings or important notes appear in a box like this.

Tips and tricks appear like this.

Reader feedback

Feedback from our readers is always welcome. Let us know what you think about this book—what you liked or may have disliked. Reader feedback is important for us to develop titles that you really get the most out of.

To send us general feedback, simply drop an email to feedback@packtpub.com, and mention the book title in the subject of your message.

If there is a book that you need and would like to see us publish, please send us a note in the **SUGGEST A TITLE** form on www.packtpub.com or email suggest@packtpub.com.

If there is a topic that you have expertise in and you are interested in either writing or contributing to a book, see our author guide on www.packtpub.com/authors.

Customer support

Now that you are the proud owner of a Packt book, we have a number of things to help you to get the most from your purchase.

Errata

Although we have taken every care to ensure the accuracy of our contents, mistakes do happen. If you find a mistake in one of our books—maybe a mistake in text or code—we would be grateful if you would report this to us. By doing so, you can save other readers from frustration and help us to improve subsequent versions of this book. If you find any errata, please report them by visiting http://www.packtpub.com/support, selecting your book, clicking on the **let us know** link, and entering the details of your errata. Once your errata are verified, your submission will be accepted and the errata added to any list of existing errata. Any existing errata can be viewed by selecting your title from http://www.packtpub.com/support.

Piracy

Piracy of copyright material on the Internet is an ongoing problem across all media. At Packt, we take the protection of our copyright and licenses very seriously. If you come across any illegal copies of our works in any form on the Internet, please provide us with the location address or web site name immediately so that we can pursue a remedy.

Please contact us at copyright@packtpub.com with a link to the suspected pirated material.

We appreciate your help in protecting our authors, and our ability to bring you valuable content.

Questions

You can contact us at questions@packtpub.com if you are having a problem with any aspect of the book, and we will do our best to address it.

1
The Skills Required to Customize Joomla!

Before we get into designing and building our new web business, it is important for us to understand how the Internet works and how Joomla! itself fits into the picture. This information will be critical to us later when we want to make changes to our site, or fix problems with it, because without this knowledge we will have little or no idea where to start.

To help us with this, we will look at:

- The architecture of the Internet
- HTML
- CSS
- Server-side scripting and PHP
- Client-side scripting with JavaScript
- Database work with MySQL and SQL

The architecture of the Internet

The Internet is primarily based off on a client/server relationship, with client computers, mostly people at home or at their office, connecting to web servers, usually as part of browsing a web site.

Because the web servers are physically separated from the client computers, and could be thousands of miles away, Internet interactions are limited to distinct requests and responses to and from web servers. It doesn't happen instantaneously, like with a native application that is running on our computer. Even though some modern web sites and high-speed connections can seem almost to act like a native application, they still operate in the same way as other web sites, via request and response.

This difference is illustrated in the following figure:

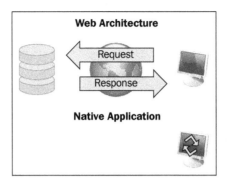

When building a web site, the web developer will put all the files needed for the site onto the web server. Then when a person on their client computer visits the web site using a web browser, they don't actually go to the site. The reality is that the *site comes to them*. The client sends their request to the web server, the web server sends them a copy of all of the web pages and files that are needed to fulfill their request, and then their web browser assembles the files into a presentable web page, as illustrated in the following figure:

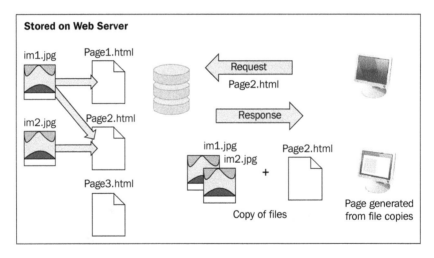

Why is this important? Because it is important to realize that when someone is interacting with our web business, they aren't interacting with it live, but only with its copy that was downloaded onto their computer. This will affect how we approach designing, building, and also fixing our web business.

Modern Internet advances, such as cloud computing, AJAX, caching, and the like have recently produced a growing number of instances that are slightly different to the model given above, or at least appear to be different. However, they all still follow the basic premise of request and response.

HTML

Originally, web pages consisted primarily of many individual files, each containing all the design information and data, and links to any images that needed to be displayed on a single viewable page. This information and data was, and still is, written in a language called HTML.

While many people refer to HTML as a programming language, it is in fact, as the name states, a markup language. That is a language that doesn't provide instructions on something to do (a program) but instead, tells how to display itself and the data it contains.

This means that HTML code by itself is not capable of actually *doing* anything except structuring and displaying static data in a certain way.

HTML works by putting the data inside tags, indicated with greater than and less than symbols, and these tags tell the reader (usually a web browser) how to organize the data structurally.

Some examples of HTML tags:

```
<h1>This is a level 1 Header</h1>
<p>This is a paragraph</p>
<div>This is a div, used to divide information into logical
  containers.</div>
<ul>
<li>A List Item (li) in an unordered list (ul).</li>
</ul>
<span>This is a span of text. </span>
```

An HTML document almost always has at least the following tags:

```
<html>
<head></head>
<body></body>
</html>
```

The `<head></head>` tags are used to hold information about the document which affects the display of the data, but does not actually get displayed on the page itself, whereas the `<body></body>` tags contain the data that is to be displayed in the web browser.

HTML can also contain extra pieces of information inside the actual tags themselves, and not just between the tags. These bits of information are called **attributes**. The extra information in these attributes is used to provide extra features and functionality to the HTML when displayed. For example, links and images need to be told where to send people when clicked, or what image to load.

```
<a href="www.awebsite.com">A link to a website</a>
<img src="www.awebsite.com/logo.jpg" />
```

We probably noticed that the image tag, `<img>`, didn't have a closing tag with a slash in it. This is because some tags can be self closed if it doesn't make sense for them to have two tags, such as with our image. To self close a tag, simply put a slash as the last character in the tag.

This is far from a complete guide to HTML, as there are dozens, if not hundreds of guides to HTML online and in book form. Please look to them for more information HTML. Also recommended is the website `www.w3schools.com` for more detailed information on HTML and its descendant, XHTML.

We can also use a `style` attribute in our HTML code to add design elements to what is otherwise only a logical structure.

```
<span style="color:red; font-weight:bold;
      background-color:yellow">It's an emergency!</span>
```

Originally, this was how most HTML was styled. However, it was quickly realized that mixing design information, structural information, and the data itself into the same file was dangerous and made updating the data difficult without affecting the design, and updating the design was difficult without potentially affecting the data. So an attempt was made to strip the design information out of the HTML files, leaving only the data and data structure in the original files, and putting the design information into separate files.

This led to what is today called cascading style sheets (CSS), separate files containing the majority of the design information for a web page:

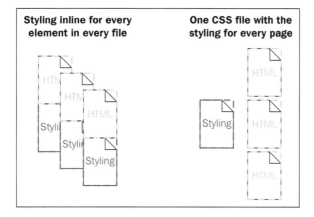

CSS

CSS is used to style the logical layout elements of HTML into attractive web sites. It differs from HTML, in that HTML organizes the data on the page into logical containers, and then CSS provides the information needed to then style these containers.

CSS is usually stored in its own file(s) separate to the main HTML document. This is to separate the styling from the logical data structure, so that one of them can be changed or altered without affecting the other, resulting in web sites that are easier to maintain.

Also, if HTML and CSS are in separate files, then one CSS file can be used for many different HTML pages, as opposed to painstakingly putting the styling into each file separately. This allows for site wide changes to the design to be done by editing only a single file. This also naturally saves disk space as well as identical styling information is no longer repeated on every page.

 There are times when the CSS code may be required to be written directly into a HTML document. Many of the reasons are the result of dynamic page generation, which we will cover soon. But at these times the CSS should be written between the `<head></head>` tags.

CSS works via referencing HTML tags and attributes and then applying styles to them.

For example, to style all of our paragraph tags, <p>, to be bold and blue, we could use the following CSS code.

```
p {
    font-weight:bold;
    color: blue;
}
```

Then, all data between any <p> tags on our page would turn bold and blue. As we can see that is much easier than typing the same thing into a style attribute on every single set of <p> tags.

However, sometimes we won't want to style all of the tags on a page identically. What if we want to only style one of our paragraphs, and to give it red text?

If we need to identify individual tags, we can use class and id attributes in our HTML to focus the target for our CSS styles. Class attributes are used for CSS that will style multiple HTML elements in the same way, and id attributes are used for CSS that will only affect unique HTML elements. In other words:

- class = More than one per page
- id = A maximum one per page

So let's return to our red paragraph and say that it is for a warning box. The chances are that our warning box will only be used once per page, but there is a possibility that it could be used more than once if there are multiple warnings. So we should choose a class for our attribute. It might look like this:

```
<p class="warningbox">Be careful when doing this!</p>
```

Now, into our CSS file we will add:

```
p.warningbox {
    color: red;
}
```

Notice how after our p we now have .warningbox. The full stop before warningbox indicates that we are after a class. If warningbox was an id, then we would use a hash symbol, #, between p and warningbox.

But what about when there are two or more declarations that overlap? Such as:

```
p {
    font-weight:bold;
    color: blue;
}
p.warningbox {
    color: red;
}
```

Do we get red or blue `<p>` tags? Are they all bold or not?

Referring back to the full name of CSS, the C in it stands for **Cascading**. This is because when several styles attempt to affect the same HTML, a set of rules are applied that give priority to certain styles, and allow others to flow down, in a logical cascade.

Generally, the cascade is dictated by the following rules, with number 4 having the highest priority:

1. Browser Default Style
2. External Style Sheet (loaded from a different file)
3. Internal Style Sheet (inside the `<head>` tag)
4. Inline Style (written in the `style` attribute in an HTML tag)

On top of these rules, the more specific a rule is, the higher its priority, with classes outranking basic HTML elements, and ids outranking classes.

So given the above rules, and looking back at our two rules for `<p>` tags listed above, the following will happen:

- All `<p>` tags on the page **without** a class of `warningbox` will be colored blue
- All `<p>` tags **with** a class of `warningbox` will override the blue color with red because it is more specific
- All `<p>` tags will be bold, **regardless of class**, as the `font-weight` style cascades down

When including CSS styles in the `<head>` tags of a document we will need to put them inside their own `<style>` tags such as:

```
<head>
    <style type="text/css">
      p {color:blue}
    </style>
</head>
```

Did we notice the `type="text/css"` attribute? This is not technically required, but is highly encouraged and recommended to future proof a web site. Not doing it is considered bad practice by many developers.

When putting CSS styles into a separate file there is no need to put `<style>` tags into the CSS file, the styles can just be written directly into the file.

However, in the HTML page we use `<link>` tags to load the external CSS file, and put these into the site header, similar to what we did above.

```
<link rel="stylesheet" type="text/css" href="/cssfile.css" />
```

Usually this tag will be used exactly as it is here and will only need the `href` attribute changed to point to the correct CSS file.

In a Joomla! site, most of our CSS references will come from one of three places, either from our site template, the frontend or admin template, or the references will come from extensions we have installed. Usually these are components, but modules and plugins can also add their own CSS references in.

As with the HTML section, this is far from a complete guide to CSS, and there are an equally large number of books and online resources available to study CSS. Also I recommended again is the website www.w3schools.com for more detailed information on HTML, and its descendant, XHTML.

CSS gives us a lot of power to style our site, and prevents the same styles from being repeated in the HTML files for every page of the site and consolidates them into one file. But what can be done about repeated HTML? Quite a lot of our site's logical structure will be identical on every page, things such as our company logo, menus, headers, advertisements, and other things all look the same on every page, so why are we wasting time and disk space recoding them over and over?

It was this last type of thinking that lead to the next step in web site evolution, "dynamically generated HTML" via "server-side scripting".

Server-side scripting and PHP

Server-side scripting is a web server technology that replaces the use of static, unchanging HTML pages with dynamically generated HTML pages. The pages are generated by scripts on the server (hence the name) when requested and passed back to the browser.

These dynamically generated pages have a number of significant benefits over static pages:

- Easier maintenance, because there is usually only a single copy of any site-wide HTML
- Content can change and react to user preferences or input
- Content can be added or changed without changing any HTML

- Sites are often constantly evolving and improving as users and developers alike add content to the site via dynamic communication technologies such as forums or comments

- Much faster to make updates to the entire site layout

There are many different languages that can be used for server-side scripting, but since Joomla! uses PHP, so we will be focusing our studies there.

A dynamic, PHP powered, site's structure differs from a static web site in several key ways:

- There is usually only one main file that is ever called from the browser, almost always named index.php, and different pages are generated according to parameters passed to the server from the client.

- Usually a database or data files of some sort are used to separate the raw data from the HTML, and they are then assembled upon the user's request.

- A PHP web site only sends generated pages to the client. Pages that do not actually exist on the server as a file in the form that the client receives them. However, most static HTML sites send exact copies of the HTML files that are on the server.

- Instead of a mass of HTML files, there are usually fewer files, and they contain mainly scripting code, and much less HTML.

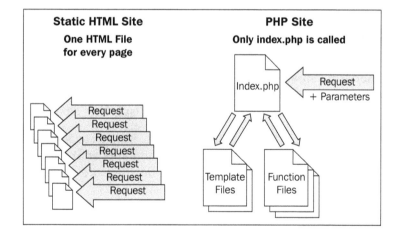

 Because PHP runs on the server, our client browser only ever downloads the already generated HTML and never sees, nor even knows about, the PHP.

Joomla!, like most PHP sites, uses the file index.php as the primary gateway to a site. This file receives the requests from the browser and then calls the appropriate PHP functions needed to create a page that matches the request. However, please note that we will usually never change any of the code inside a Joomla! site's index.php file because all it does is call other files, many of these are template or extension files. It is the template and extension PHP files that we will usually be editing.

> Joomla! templates also include an index.php file. This index.php file and the Joomla! core index.php file are different and serve different purposes. Editing a template's index.php file is a very common practice, unlike the core Joomla! file. Be careful when you start opening any index.php files to make sure you are editing the right one.

As mentioned above, most PHP generated sites, including Joomla! use a database to store their raw data. This makes it much easier, and faster, to retrieve data when it is requested by the user. It also allows powerful data operations and functions to be performed on the data if needed, such as aggregating it, sorting it, or making it easier to read.

The most common database for PHP sites, and the one used by Joomla! is MySQL. It is popular because not only is it open source and requires no cost to download and install, but it is also very reliable and powerful.

PHP code is designed to operate in two main methods. First, it can be run as complete PHP file. Usually these files are used for data processing, function declarations, or other unseen work.

The other method is to embed PHP into HTML code, usually to add loops, conditions, and load data into the otherwise static HTML, and usually these mixed HTML/PHP files are used as templates, or parts of templates, for displaying data on a site.

PHP can be easily recognized by the telltale <?php ... ?> tags around sections of code. These tags are needed to complete PHP files and appear at the very start and end of the file. However, in a mixed HTML/PHP file, there are usually many, shorter code sections and tags.

> PHP is a detailed and complex language and there is no way we could cover it in any usable detail in this chapter. Instead, it is recommended again that you find some of the many great online and offline resources. One of the best sites to get PHP information is www.php.net, which contains a complete list of the available functions and commands for PHP. You can also pick up one of the great PHP books from Packt Publishing (www.packtpub.com/php-mysql)

The basic operation of a Joomla! site revolves around the `index.php` file, calling the PHP files for the extensions and template required by the client request, and then assembling the HTML code output by them into a page and then sending it to the client. Extension PHP files usually reside in a `/components/com_componentname` directory, `/modules/mod_modulename`, or `/plugin/plugintype/plg_pluginname` and templates in a `/templates/templatename` folder.

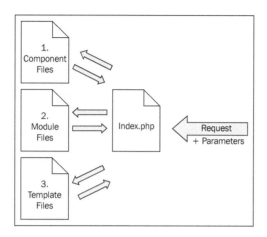

 Plugins were not included in the preceding diagram because they execute at many different times throughout the site.

MVC programming and PHP

From Joomla! 1.5, the PHP code architecture has been converted into what is called a **Model-View-Controller (MVC)** architecture. MVC is an attempt to separate business logic from data and from the user interface, with the model representing the data, the view representing the user interface, and the controller representing the business logic.

This is easily seen with Joomla! Extensions, which will often have `model`, `view`, and `controller` subfolders containing the relevant MVC PHP files for that extension.

The files in the `view` folders are most likely to have PHP and embedded HTML files, and the `model` and `controller` folders should only contain fully PHP files.

 For more information about PHP and MVC within Joomla! extensions, I highly recommend the book *Joomla! Extension Development*, also from Packt Publishing.

PHP does have limitations though. Its dynamically generated pages still look fairly static by the time they reach the client, and PHP operates on the server, so what do we do if we want some dynamic activities on the client?

This question brings us to client-side scripting, and JavaScript.

Client-side scripting and JavaScript

Client-side scripting was designed to fill a similar purpose to server-side scripting, to add dynamic features to otherwise static HTML pages, but with a completely different target. Where server-side scripting is used to make the **generation of** HTML dynamic, client-side scripting is used to make the **interaction with** HTML dynamic. This operation is conveniently referred to as **Dynamic HTML or DHTML**.

DHTML refers to anything constructed out of HTML which is then animated, updated, re-colored or otherwise changed in some fashion via scripting languages such as JavaScript or VBScript. It is the power behind many tabs, slideshows, sliding menus, validation for forms, and much more.

In the same way that Joomla! uses PHP for its server-side scripting, it also uses JavaScript for its client-side scripting. So we will place our focus on understanding how JavaScript works.

Similar to CSS, JavaScript, often just called **JS**, can either be entered directly into a HTML document or loaded from an external file which is the preferred method. The main differences are in the syntax for doing so.

Where CSS uses `<style>` tags, JS uses `<script>` tags when entering it into an HTML file, as shown:

```
<head>
   <script type="text/javascript">
      var someVariable = "a value";
   </script>
</head>
```

Notice how we have entered the `type` attribute again, only this time it says `text/javascript` and not `text/css`.

When loading external JS files, the syntax is also similar, but different, to CSS.

```
<script type="text/javascript" src="myJSScript.js"></script>
```

Unlike CSS, which has different tags for loading external files and entering directly into the HTML file `<link>` and `<style>` respectively, JS uses the same tags, `<script>`, for both operations. The main difference being that external files are loaded by adding a `src` attribute to the tags, indicating **source**, which contains the address of the required JS file.

JS is just as detailed and complex a language as PHP, so again it is recommended that you find some of the many great online and offline resources. One of the best sites to get JS information is one you will already be familiar with, www.w3schools.com. Or, alternatively, pick up one of the many great JS books also from Packt Publishing (www.packtpub.com/ajax)

Asynchronous JavaScript and XML (AJAX)

AJAX, is an Internet buzzword that many people will be familiar with but few understand it properly. Many people attribute moving and sliding elements on a web site to AJAX, when in reality these are usually just DHTML. AJAX, in reality, refers to a process of making requests to the server, usually via something called the `XMLHttpRequest` object, in the background to send or retrieve data to and from the web server without having to reload the entire page. This is the normal practice for a web site.

For example, a set of tabs that loads all the data at the same time as the page loads and then shows them one at a time is DHTML.

But a set of tabs that dynamically loads the data for each tab one at a time from the server, *after* the page has already loaded, and *when* the tab in question is selected by the user is AJAX (and DHTML for the actual showing/hiding of the tabs).

AJAX offers several advantages for web sites:

- Initial page load times are reduced as not all data is needed up front
- Interaction with the page seems faster as new information can be grabbed on request, without full page reloads
- The pages feel more like a native application with live feedback than a web site with a fixed request/response system

But it also carries some disadvantages:

- Page changes aren't usually recorded in the browser history, so hitting the **Back** button on the browser may produce unexpected behavior
- Disabled visitors, or visitors without JS enabled may not be able to use the site properly
- Search engines may not be able to index the site properly as they can't record all the changes

Because of these disadvantages, there is a consensus among many professional developers today that JS and AJAX should be used sparingly, and for enhancement of sites that can operate without it, and not as an essential part of the site operation.

JavaScript frameworks—Mootools and jQuery

In web programming terms, a **framework** is a collection of prewritten program code designed to make it easier to develop using the language that the framework is designed for. The prewritten code usually contains many functions that bundle up more difficult commands needed to do common activities, and makes them far simpler to perform.

These frameworks generally lower the entry barrier for using those languages, and allow less skilled developers to produce far more powerful web sites than they could otherwise.

In the Joomla! community, there are two main **JavaScript frameworks** that are widely used. The first one is **Mootools**, which is also included by default in Joomla! 1.5, and is used by many of the larger template clubs. The second is **jQuery**, a framework favored by many extension developers (though many also use Mootools).

Mootools is most apparent initially on a Joomla! site in the administrator side. Where the accordion effect appears on the right-hand side modules in the control panel, the pop-ups for parameter screens, the attractive tooltips around the site, and more are all thanks to Mootools.

Generally, frameworks don't play well together and the end result of loading two or more on a page is usually that none of them work and all our JS fails. Luckily, however, the jQuery team implemented some commands known as **no-conflict mode**, which has allowed jQuery to operate alongside other frameworks without a conflict.

The frameworks generally consist of one or more JavaScript files which are loaded onto our page like normal JavaScript. After loading these scripts, we are free to call the functions from these frameworks and use them in our own JavaScript, saving us time and effort.

One of the main drawbacks with frameworks is that they are almost always going to be larger than we need and include functions that we are never going to use. This can affect our site performance, as we will discuss later.

The other main drawback, as noted above, is that of potential conflicts. Personally, the largest single support problem I encounter in my day-to-day work is without a doubt because of JavaScript framework conflicts. In the later chapter, we will cover how we can determine if a JavaScript framework has caused our site problems, and how to diagnose and fix those problems.

 More information about Mootools and jQuery can be found at their respective sites, `http://mootools.net` and `http://jquery.com`. Also there are many useful titles available at `http://www.packtpub.com/ajax`.

Database work with MySQL and SQL

Jumping back to the server, an understanding the technologies behind Joomla! can't be considered complete without a discussion on **Structured Query Language (SQL)**. SQL is the language of choice for most databases, and anytime we want to add or retrieve data from the database of a Joomla! site, we will need to do it via SQL.

SQL is a relatively straightforward and simple language to pick up, but it can get quite complex at higher levels of development. It is designed purely to interact with data in a database and can do very little else.

The four most common SQL commands we will use are:

- `SELECT`
- `INSERT`
- `UPDATE`
- `DELETE`

There are others, but these are the ones we will need to know most.

Following one of these initial commands will usually be a preposition and a table name. Or it could be a comma separated list of columns, then the proposition and table name and is written in fairly easy to understand language. For example:

```
SELECT name, address FROM person_table …
INSERT INTO person_table …
UPDATE person_table …
DELETE FROM person_table …
```

For SELECT, UPDATE, and DELETE, there will also usually be a WHERE clause that provides the criteria upon which to do the search.

```
SELECT name, address FROM person_table WHERE age > "16"
UPDATE person_table … WHERE name = "John Doe"
DELETE FROM person_table WHERE name = "John Doe"
```

For INSERT queries, there will also be a set of values to insert, and possibly a list of columns to INSERT INTO.

```
INSERT INTO person_table (name, address, age)
VALUES ( "John Doe","10 This St, Atown","25")
```

For UPDATE queries, they are again a little different, but easy to understand.

```
UPDATE person_table SET address="25 Anew St, Atown"
WHERE  name = "John Doe"
```

Something we will sometimes see with SELECT statements is the use of an asterix (*) character in place of a column list. This is shorthand to indicate that we want to use all of the available columns, arranged in the same order as they appear in the database.

```
SELECT * FROM person_table WHERE age > "16"
```

Something we will quickly notice if we are looking over existing Joomla! database queries is that almost all of them will have a hash and two underscores before the table name. For example:

```
SELECT * FROM #__person_table
```

This hash underscore is replaced at run time with the current database prefix. So #__person_table will be converted into something similar to jos_person_table by the Joomla! database functions when they run the query.

The database prefix exists to allow people to install multiple Joomla! sites and use the same database for all of them, without the data for each one overwriting the others. The different sites can then just use different prefixes, and that way they keep all their data in separate tables.

As with all of our programming topics, there is a lot more useful information available on the Internet regarding MySQL and the SQL programming language (sites such as `http://www.w3schools.com/SQl/default.asp`).

Summary

We should by now have a basic understanding of the main technologies and programming languages used by a Joomla! site. Enough at least to allow us to tell the difference between a CSS file and a JavaScript file, between PHP and HTML, and so on.

It is strongly recommended that anyone serious about his or her site take their studies of these technologies further and builds up their skills with them. Even if they themselves are not going to do most of the development, perhaps they have hired developers for example, understanding these things will still make communicating with those developers much easier.

2
Setting Up Our Environment

When fixing a car, would you use an axe and a chainsaw? When building a house would you do it with a toothbrush and a bottle opener? The answer to both of these questions is an easy no. We all know that you need the right tools for the job, otherwise you risk accidents, the chance that it won't be finished properly, or possibly even finished at all.

It is the same with building a web site. The better the tools, the easier and faster you can work, and the greater the end result will be. So, before we get into building our site, we are going to take a look at some of the available tools and applications for Joomla! developers, and how to use them effectively to improve our performance.

Our goals for this chapter:

- Learn about the different categories of tools available
- Look at several tools for our own use, depending on our budget and the type of computer we use—Windows/Mac
- Become comfortable with the basic usage of some our chosen tools

Before we even start looking at our site, it's best that we have our environment completely setup. Why? Because it becomes more difficult to change our environment as our work progresses. We start to form habits that are difficult to change, we may make mistakes that are difficult to fix, or we may simply waste the time that could have been saved by doing things correctly from the start.

Types of tools

There are many, many great tools out there for developers, but most developers will usually have at least one tool from each of the following seven categories:

- A file transfer application
- A program code editor

- An image editor
- Several web browsers
- A database management tool
- A source code repository to store code
- A local web server

File transfers

File transfer applications are essential, because web site developers will always need to be able to copy files over the Internet and up to their server, whether it's program code, images, movies, or any other type of files. Most file transfer applications use a method called **File Transfer Protocol (FTP)** to send files to and receive files from their site. So the first tools we are going to look at are FTP applications, also called **FTP clients**.

 Many FTP clients, include the letters FTP, or the word File somewhere in their name, making them usually easy to recognize.

One very popular and free FTP client is **FileZilla**, available from `filezilla-project.org`. FileZilla has a straightforward interface, and is available on both the Mac and Windows platform, so it is easy to recommend it.

For the Mac people out there, **Transmit**, a commercial FTP client from the team at `www.panic.com/transmit`, is another solid choice. Transmit has a very easy to use interface, and will immediately feel familiar to Mac users, because of its similarity to the native Mac finder.

Not to forget our Windows brothers and sisters who want something more, I personally prefer **WS_FTP** from `ipswitch.com`. It's a little more powerful than FileZilla in several respects, and I feel that it has a nicer interface.

When sending information via FTP, we will usually be presented with two options for the method—ASCII and Binary—in which we send the data.

ASCII is used for transferring information in character form and should only be used for data that is only text (for example, programming code), as it will corrupt any non-text data, such as images or executable files. It is useful when transferring documents between different operating systems as most FTP clients will automatically convert things like end of line characters and special characters to the equivalent character on the destination server.

Binary sends our data, as the name implies, in binary format so it is safe for any type of data. Binary should be used for any non-text transfers, but can be used safely for text documents as well, though no character substitution will take place.

Code editing

Probably the most difficult, and important tool to get right is the code editor or **Integrated Development Environment (IDE)**. Picking the right IDE is important because it will be one of the tools we will use the most when working on our site, especially as our programming skills grow. Using the right IDE can save us hours or even days of work when developing.

A good IDE will usually have at least the following two features:

- **Code highlighting**: Different types of code (variables, functions, and so on) are colored differently, making it easier to read and spot mistakes.
- **Auto completion**: When you type the first few letters of a command, function, or keyword it offers a list of suggestions to choose from, saving time and preventing mistakes.

There are lots of other features available, but these are the two features that most developers would consider essential in their IDE.

One of the top IDEs around, **Eclipse** (www.eclipse.org), also happens to be free and open source, making it a good choice for many developers. This is further supported by the fact that it is available for both Mac and Windows PCs. It also supports a dizzying variety of plugins that we can use to add new features to it. When developing a Joomla! site, we will want to find and install at least the **PHPEclipse** (www.phpeclipse.com) plugin to allow us to edit Joomla! Extensions, and core Joomla! files properly.

One disadvantage for eclipse is that it is a little complex (because it is also very powerful) and may overwhelm inexperienced developers. To get around this, I personally recommend using **Aptana Studio** (http://aptana.com/), which is based on eclipse and also runs in almost the exact same way, accepting the same plugins, and so on. However, it has been subtly enhanced to be more user-friendly, and comes with the most common plugins that a Joomla! developer would want already pre installed. These plugins can be easily added with a single click. They also include many tutorials on their site, in the support section, to help new developers understand, and use Eclipse/Aptana Studio.

Another excellent editor that is available on both Windows and Mac is Adobe Dreamweaver (www.adobe.com/products/dreamweaver/). This commercial IDE is aimed at web development in general and not just at HTML and PHP. It has all the features we would expect in a modern IDE and is used by many developers.

Another free IDE, **PSPad** (www.pspad.com), is also a good choice for beginning Windows developers, as it is quite simple to use and has an interface similar to a word processor. It does, however, lack an auto completion functionality, which is its only major drawback. Many experienced developers also use PSPad, because it is very lightweight and fast, even when handling large files.

For Windows users who can afford it, **PHPed** (www.nusphere.com) is highly recommended as it is focused on PHP web development (unlike Eclipse, Dreamweaver, and PSPad which are general IDEs), and even has a Joomla! plugin for its auto completion engine. Thus, giving us access to functions from Joomla! itself, without having to remember them.

For Mac users, there are quite a few good IDEs out there. However, two, in particular, stand out from the crowd. First is **Coda** (www.panic.com/coda), touted as *one window web development*. Coda not only has the standard IDE features, but also includes an FTP client, an SVN client (which we will talk about later), a built-in technical book library, and several other great and useful features for web developers. This is the IDE that we will see used in all the demos throughout the book as it is one of the best to work with.

Another great IDE for Mac is **CSSEdit** (macrabbit.com). Unfortunately, it is focused solely on CSS, and does not support HTML or PHP at all, and so it has only a limited scope for developers, but it is nonetheless recommended as one of the best CSS IDEs around.

Image editing

A good image editor is another important tool for a developer. These, however, are harder to come by without paying a hefty price in either money or practice.

Gimp (www.gimp.org) is a popular free image replacement program, but it has quite a steep learning curve, one that I personally never took the time to climb, preferring other editors. Many developers, however, swear by it, as it is, without a doubt, the most powerful free editor available, and is conveniently available on both Mac and Windows.

A program derived from the Mac version of Gimp, called **Seashore** (seashore.sourceforge.net), is also available for free to all Mac users. While it has a simpler interface, it is significantly less powerful than Gimp.

Many people use **Adobe Photoshop** (www.adobe.com), but like Gimp, it also has a fairly steep learning curve to get professional results. There are however, thousands of tutorials out there for it to help people get started.

The top preference of many web designers is **Adobe Fireworks**—formerly Macromedia Fireworks (`www.adobe.com`). It is similar to both Photoshop and Adobe Illustrator, but without the complexity of either of them. It has been specifically designed for working with images for the Web, unlike Photoshop (for photos) or Illustrator (for large vector print design and illustrations). It is very easy to pick up to begin producing and editing images that look professional within just a few hours. It is, unfortunately, quite expensive, so may be out of the price range of many beginner developers, but is highly recommended for anyone serious about web development or design.

Web browsing

A common mistake that many new developers make when starting out is assuming that everyone uses the same web browser as them. The truth is that our site visitors will probably come to us from any number of browsers. "Why does this matter?", I hear you ask. Well, we should test our site in as many browsers as possible, as they all have different ways of handling web pages. Our site may look great in Firefox, for example, but look like a dog's breakfast in Internet Explorer.

Testing in a wide variety of browsers helps us to ensure that as many people as possible can access our site and our products.

The recommended browsers that we should test with as a minimum are:

- Internet Explorer 6
- Internet Explorer 7
- Internet Explorer 8 (not as important as 6 and 7 though)
- Firefox (`www.mozilla.com/firefox`)
- Opera (`www.opera.com`)
- Safari (`www.apple.com/safari`)
- Google Chrome (`www.google.com/chrome`)

Usually, if your site looks good in Safari, Opera, Firefox, or Chrome, then there is a good chance that it will look fine in the others in that list since all of them support CSS standards quite well, and usually only require slight tweaks to get them looking good.

Internet Explorer, however, is totally different. Generally, it is considered very difficult to work with by most web developers, because of its lack of support, and non standard support, for CSS standards. Internet Explorer, particularly versions 6 and 7, none the less still make up over half of the traffic on the internet because for many inexperienced computer users, or people using their computer at work, Internet Explorer is the only browser they are able to use. As a result, developers will need to ensure their site works in Internet Explorer as well as other browsers.

Installing multiple browsers is as easy as downloading them and running the installer. Except for Internet Explorer, where (because we will need to install different versions) we need to first install Internet Explorer and then a program called Multiple IE (tredosoft.com/Multiple_IE), thereby allowing us to install many previous versions of Internet Explorer from 3.0 to 6.0. Really, we only need to install versions 6 and 7 for most of our testing.

For Mac users, getting Internet Explorer follows the same procedure, except that we will need to use a program such as **Parallels** (www.parallels.com) or **BootCamp** (www.apple.com/macosx/features/bootcamp.html) that allows to us to run Windows itself on our Mac machine.

A question many people have at this point is which browser should we use every day when developing?

For many web developers, the browser of choice for the bulk development is Firefox. Not because it is a better browser in itself, Safari and Chrome are both faster, and Opera has nicer core features, but because Firefox supports an extensive array of plugins, in particular one called **Firebug** (www.getfirebug.com) which allows real time editing and testing of web pages. Thus, reducing the testing and development time dramatically for the front-end of our web site.

There are also many other great plugins for Firefox to support web developers, another favorite being the **Web Developer Toolbar** (chrispederick.com/work/web-developer) that contains many useful functions for developers, such as clearing specific parts of the browser cache, turning JavaScript on and off, and more.

Microsoft has also released an **Internet Explorer Developer Toolbar** that does significantly reduce the headaches of working with Internet Explorer, however it is not nearly as useful as Firebug.

Database administration

Being database-driven, it is important to be able to access and alter the database for a Joomla! site. There may come times that we need to fix data, or perform testing and the only way is to get into the database itself.

By far, the most popular database administration tool is **phpMyAdmin** (www.phpmyadmin.net), a web-based database management tool provided free of cost by most major web hosts. phpMyAdmin is not a perfect database administration tool, but it does more than is required by most web site developers, so is a good choice.

Usually phpMyAdmin will be preinstalled on our web server. If by some chance it is not and we want to install it ourselves, or we simply need some more information about it, there is extensive documentation on the phpMyAdmin site (http://www.phpmyadmin.net/documentation/).

Apart from external applications, there are also some great Joomla! components that work as excellent database administration tools. One of the more flexible of these is **EasySQL** that allows us to enter our own database commands right from our site administrator panel. It is not for a novice, however, as we need to hand-write those commands.

Storing code

A source code repository is a place to store a copy of not only our code, but also the history of changes made to it, allowing us to move backwards and forwards through the changes we have made.

While not essential, having a source code repository can make developing a site, especially when working with a team, a lot smoother and easier.

A source code repository can usually be updated to and downloaded from remotely, allowing people working at different locations, or even one person who works from multiple machines, to stay updated with the latest code versions.

On top of this, most allow two people working on the same piece of code to work independently and then merge their changes together instead of having to wait for each other to finish before they can do their own work.

Probably the best benefit is the ability to have a safe, offsite backup of our site and customized code in case something goes wrong. With the added ability to go backward in time to an earlier version of the site in case some changes we just made happen to break everything.

Probably the most popular source code repository available today is **Subversion**, however, another newcomer called **Git** has been gaining popularity. We will focus mainly on Subversion though, as it is the easiest to work with for new developers.

Subversion is often referred to as SVN, and SVN repositories can be set up in one of the following three ways:

- We can do it ourselves on our web server, (preferably separate to your main server)
- We can find a web host that includes subversion as part of its offering to customers
- We can use one of several web services that provide free or paid subversion hosting

Unless we are an experienced server admin, option one is probably not for us. Option two is much less complicated, but can still be a challenge for some people, and option three is the simplest and easiest to manage for most people, however it is usually the most expensive.

SVN web services can be found both alone, such as `springloops.com`, and sometimes packaged with project management web services, such as `unfuddle.com`.

Accessing and using our SVN repository will require a client tool of some sort to be installed on our PC. We can work with SVN via a command line if we wish, but for most of us that is a very slow, cumbersome, and error prone process, so a clean graphical interface is the better option.

One of the better SVN clients is a plugin for the Eclipse IDE called **Subclipse** (`subclipse.tigris.org`), which allows us to manage our repository from inside Eclipse itself. As Eclipse is available on both Mac and Windows, and both Eclipse and the Subclipse extensions are free, this is a great choice for many people. Subclipse can also be installed into Aptana studio, which I mentioned earlier, via the easy to use plugin installer.

For Windows, there is also another great choice. **Tortoise SVN** (`tortoisesvn.tigris.org`), which is also a free application and that plugs into our file explorer in Windows and lets us manage our SVN repository from our normal file manager window.

For Mac users there is **Versions** (`www.versionsapp.com`), a new repository client that is quite solid and reliable. We may remember that I mentioned a built-in SVN client above in the IDE section. The IDE in question was Coda, and it includes a basic, but more than adequate, SVN client in their tool, making it very convenient as we can save a file and commit it to the repository without changing applications.

As the different clients all implement SVN 's functions differently in their user interfaces, it would be difficult to give a useful demonstration without showing all of the different clients. But it is useful that we understand the basic concepts used by SVN, as these concepts can be used across all the clients. In addition, an excellent web book about Subversion can be found at `http://svnbook.red-bean.com/`. This book contains a lot of excellent extra material about using Subversion.

Checkout

When we checkout an SVN repository or folder, we take a copy of it from the repository and put it onto our local computer, and set up all the files and directories needed to manage that copy on our computer. This is the very first thing we need to do before we can work with any SVN repository. Even a brand new, empty repository must be checked out to create the environment on our local computer.

A checked out repository will always need to be provided with a folder on our local machine. Everything inside this folder then becomes part of the repository.

 We will need to create a repository on our main server before we can check it out. Most of the SVN web services provide pre-created repositories or easy to use wizards to create them.

Update

We perform updates for already checked out repositories when there are some changes on the main SVN server that aren't yet present in our checked out repository. Issuing this command will cause those changed files to be downloaded and they will then be added to the right folder (new files) or replace an existing file (changed files).

Commit

Committing is the act of sending our changed, new, and deleted files and folders up to the main SVN repository on our server. Then other members of our team can download these changes by updating their local checked out copy.

Every time we commit, we create a revision which contains information about the files we changed, and the actual changes we made to them.

Add

When we want to put a file in our repository, we first copy or create it inside the folder that we checked out from our repository. Then we issue the add command to have the file included in our SVN repository.

Delete

As the name implies, this allows us to remove a file from our repository. The file will, however, not be permanently deleted, and can still be reverted as described below.

Revert

Reverting is when we take a specified revision and then copy it down to our local checked out copy, overwriting whatever changes we have made since the revision. This functions to give us what is effectively an *undo*. This is one of the key benefits of SVN, the ability to revert back to a previous version of a file if we want to undo our changes.

Ignore

There are some files that we don't want to add to subversion. For example, a configuration file that is environment-specific, as we want a different file on every server.

In these cases, we can mark a file to be ignored by SVN. This way it won't appear in commits or reverts.

 Folders in which there is a checked out repository, contain a hidden .svn folder that contains files with information about the repository, and allows the SVN clients to determine which files have changed, which are new, and so on. If we are sending files to people outside of SVN, we should make sure that we remove these hidden files before we zip up any folders. Firstly, because they take up space, and secondly because they can cause issues for the other person if they put the files we send into their own SVN directories.

Building locally

Using certain programs, it is possible to install a ready to use web server on our PC that we can develop and test our Joomla! web site on. This can take the place of using a fully fledged web server at a hosting company.

Using this local server, instead of a live web site, is the development area of choice for many Joomla! developers because of several strong advantages:

- We don't need to worry about having our site open to being hacked or people seeing our new ideas/mistakes/bugs while developing
- The site loads much faster than a remote site, speeding up the development

- File transfers are faster

- It is easier to control and change the server settings, giving more ability to find and fix problems in the code

- We can work on it even if we don't have a live internet connection

For Windows users, **Xampp** (`www.apachefriends.org/en/xampp.html`) is a popular choice for setting up a local server. Their site provides lots of information on how to setup and configure our web server.

For Mac users, **Mamp** (`www.mamp.info`) is the tool of choice for setting up a web server. There is a great instructional video provided on their home page that will help us get up and running in no time at all.

If we are setting up a local development environment, either via Xampp, Mamp, or by ourselves, there are three things we will need:

- PHP installed on our machine

- MySQL installed, and at least one database created

- Apache, or some other web server software installed

These all come by default with Xampp and Mamp, and using one of them is almost always the best option for anyone but an expert.

If we decide to develop locally, once we have finished with our site we will need to move it to our real web server. The best way to do this is via a component called JoomlaPack (`www.joomlapack.net/`). JoomlaPack will package our site into a zip file that we can then unzip onto our server and when we visit the site, it will automatically show us an installer that is almost identical to the default Joomla! installer.

The main difference being that it will install our site exactly as it was on our local development machine, extensions, content database, and everything else.

Practical—picking our tools

I have listed quite a few good tools above, now it's time to pick a set of tools for ourselves before we continue further. Having the right development environment from the start is much easier than trying to change half-way through development.

The rest of the examples in this book will be based mainly around my own environment, but all of them will be achievable regardless of the environment you choose.

The only exception to this is Firefox and Firebug. I cannot emphasis enough how important this one tool will be to the development of a site, and as of the time of writing there is no other tool that can achieve quite the same results as it can as easily.

Demonstration environment:

- PC Operating System: **Macintosh OSX**
- File Transfer / FTP Client: **Coda** + **Transmit**
- Program Code Editor / IDE: **Coda**
- Image Editor: **Adobe Fireworks**
- Primary Web Browser: Firefox + Firebug + Web Developer Toolbar
- Database Management: phpMyAdmin + EasySQL
- Source Code / SVN Repository: Unfuddle.com
- Source Code / SVN Client: Coda and Versions
- Local Web Server: Mamp

If we don't think we need them, we can leave out the SVN and local web server, but otherwise, we should ensure that we have at least one tool available for each of the remaining categories before we move on.

Practical—using our tools

As mentioned above, Firebug is a very important addition to the web developer's toolkit, but it is one that not many people will have used. Most of the other tools are fairly intuitive to use at a basic level, but Firebug needs a slight introduction.

Inspect Element

The first and most important feature of Firebug is the **Inspect Element** feature. This feature can be accessed by right-clicking on any HTML element on the page and selecting **Inspect Element** from the context menu.

Let's visit the Packt Publishing homepage (`http://www.packtpub.com`) and try it out.

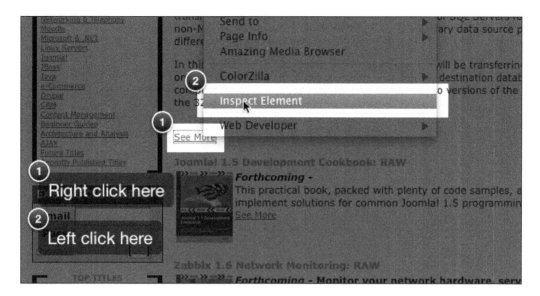

When we click the **Inspect Element** menu item, a new area should appear at the bottom of our page the looks like the next screenshot. The area that appears will usually be broken into two panes, our HTML structure on the left, and CSS information on the right. The item we selected with our right-click will be highlighted in blue, and the CSS styles applied to it will appear in the right pane.

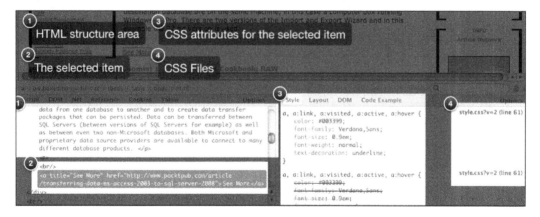

Some of the CSS styles may be crossed out. This indicates that there are two or more styles attempting to control a certain attribute of our selected item, such as the color, font-size, weight, and family in the preceding screenshot.

Obviously a piece of text can't have two colors or font sizes simultaneously, so only the highest priority CSS styles are displayed if two or more try to control the same attribute.

We will discuss how to change the priority of CSS styles later, but for now understand that only the styles which aren't crossed out are being applied to our item.

Scrolling up and down the CSS list to the right, we can see all of the styles applied to our item, as well as the file, and even the line number from where these styles come from. This allows us to quickly see what files and what styles we need to change if we want to change the appearance of the selected item.

This is already immensely useful to a web developer, but it only gets better from here. Let's imagine that we want to change the color of all links on the Packt web site to a different color. We could open up the files listed, type in our new color, save the files, and copy them up to our server. We could then reload the page in order to test it. If we don't like the changes, we have to do the same process again and again and again until we get it right.

Wouldn't it be great if we could test our changes before making them? Well we can!

In the CSS window to the right, click on the value for the top most color attribute (the one not crossed out). Upon doing so, the value will seem to pop out of the page a little and we will be able to edit it as shown in the following screenshot:

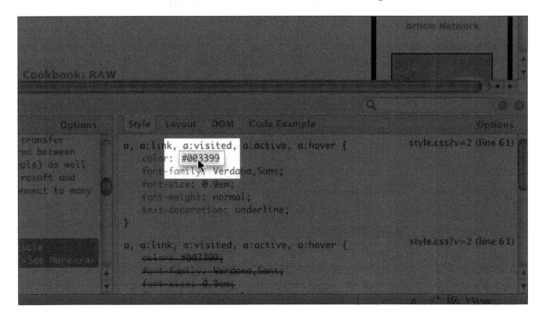

Type #33FF00 into the value box and look at our links again. We should see something like the following:

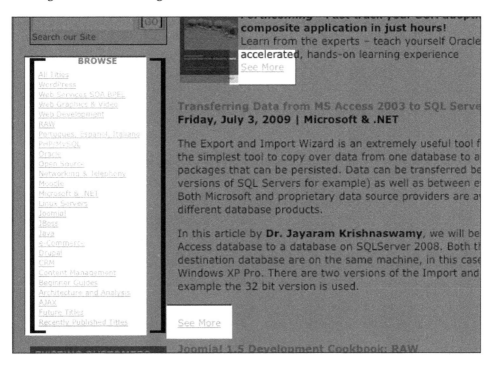

Take some time to play around, selecting different items and changing attributes, and see what we can do to the site. Notice that if we reload the page, everything goes back to how it was? This is because we are only changing the site in our browser, not back on the server. So for our own sites, we will still need to make the changes to the CSS files and upload them to our server. This gives us the ability test and refine our changes live in the browser before we make them permanent.

We may have also noticed that as we move the mouse around the left-hand panel that shows the HTML structure, sections on the main web site will change color. These changes help us identify what each item in the HTML structure looks like on the page.

The three main colors that appear are light blue, purple, and yellow as we can see in the next screenshot. The light blue represents the basic item itself, the purple represents any padding that has been applied to the item, and the yellow represents margins.

This color-coding helps us see, at a glance, how things on our site are spaced.

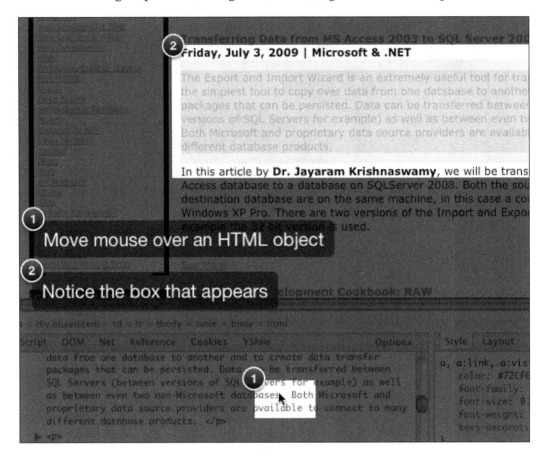

This is just the beginning of what is possible with Firebug, but is enough to get us started and prepared for the later chapters where we will work on our site. Later, we will cover how to debug JavaScript and other useful features of Firebug.

Summary

So we should now be well on our way to getting set up to start work on our site. We have looked at the different categories of tools we need, and some of the many tools available in those categories, and we also looked at how to use one of the more useful tools, Firebug. We should also have decided upon and acquired the tools we wish to use when working on our site.

So now let's move onto planning for our site.

3
Planning Our Site

One of the most important steps in building our site is the planning stage. This stage is often poorly executed because:

- we often want to get right into building our site immediately
- it starts out as a hobby, or practice site and slowly grows into our business
- we plan our site based on the extensions we want, rather than basing the extensions we want off the plan for our site

It is, however, vitally important to properly plan our site before we start building it if we ultimately want it to be successful and not simply a domain, a collection of extensions, and a template drifting lost in cyberspace.

If we are hoping to build a real business out of our site, it is especially important to plan it out properly because our site's success and failure translates directly into income or no income.

While we are planning, we are also going to put some thought into how we are going to structure our business income, look at the options available to us, and then choose one or more that are appropriate to our mission and goals.

So, in this chapter we aim to cover:

- why it is so important to plan
- how to write the mission statement and goals
- decide how our site will generate income
- how to pick extensions based on our goals
- what are some of the basic *must have* extensions for most Joomla! sites
- the goals and extensions for our sample site

Why is it so important to plan?

Planning is important firstly because it keeps us on the right path towards our goal, and secondly it helps us keep our site clean and simple and not succumb to what I call the "Frankensite" effect.

The Frankensite effect

Imagine building a house simply by finding random pieces of nice house fittings, some floor coverings that caught our eye, bathroom and kitchen fittings, doors, and door handles. All of these items picked individually without any thought for the style, size, or appearance of the other items. Then, after we have all the parts we want, finding a block of land, and assembling all the pieces randomly without any plan of what kind of house we want.

I am sure you can imagine the crazy, monstrous house that would result. To do this with a house would be unthinkable for most people.

Many people, however, build their web sites, and even their business in this way. They collect a big list of extensions they want to use and then try to work out what kind of site they can build from them. In some cases, not even *that much* planning is done and they just add extension after extension to the site without considering the site appearance or functionality.

This is what I like to call a Frankensite. Just like the legendary monster made by doctor Frankenstein, a Frankensite doesn't look like, nor behave like, a professional web business. Rather, it looks more like a collection of extensions stitched together by a mad scientist in a grotesque, terrifying parody of one.

Well, I am sorry to break it to those people, but they are *not* the first person to think that installing Community Builder, SOBI, JEvents, Groupjive, a forum component, and all 50 plus plugins for them will somehow give them a Facebook killer, nor will they be the last.

I would be confident in saying that this is one of the single biggest reasons that many CMS-based sites (not just Joomla!) fail, or only experience mediocre success. It is very easy to install Joomla!, slap on a template, and install every extension we can find. But if we wish to actually succeed and keep customers and visitors on our site, we need to build trust and provide a simple and useful service or information. Mashing extensions into a site with no planning just makes the site confusing, difficult to navigate, and ultimately unusable for most, if not all people. The end result is a lack of trust and people leaving us, never to return.

Having too many extensions also makes it very difficult to style a site properly. Especially, if those extensions already have fixed styling which we can't change (such as flash extensions) or are difficult to style (no CSS files, just elements hard coded into the HTML itself). This inability to style effectively is what gives a Frankensite their characteristic stitched together look. Different fonts, sizes, colors, lines, buttons, and styling all combine to make the site look like a monster and not a respectable business.

Ultimately, we want our web site to look as little like a Joomla! site as possible. The less it looks like a bunch of unrelated extensions patched together and the more it looks like a cohesive well designed site, the more easily our customers will come to trust us and the more successful we will be. The best way to achieve this result is through detailed planning.

Remember though that while appearances certainly aren't everything, and we need to have substance in our site to actually keep people, we get only one chance to make that critical first impression and get our visitors to take the time to inspect our site.

No one can hit a target they don't have

Besides the Frankensite effect, building a site without planning is like driving in the fog through a forest. We have no idea where we are going, and are only able to see a few feet in front of ourselves. We can't actually get anywhere, and all we can do is try to dodge problems when they appear, or fix the car if we do hit a problem. Many poorly planned web sites also end up like this. They are never able to really go forward, they merely try to avoid, and fix, the problems they come across.

This is because, if we don't plan our site carefully, we won't have any idea what it is we are actually trying to build. What service or product is it we are providing? Who are we providing it to? Why should they buy it from us and not someone else?

We can't market our site if we don't know what it is meant to be doing, and if we can't market our site, then our visitors are going to have a hard time finding us.

Also, if we have a plan with clear goals for our site, then whenever we need to make a decision we can compare any questions, decisions, or problems that arise with our goals and decide which answer moves us closer to them. This makes the whole process quicker and smoother.

With a good plan, we will also find that the development time is sped up and our site will go live faster, allowing us to bring in more customers, and thus more income.

If we have dozens of extensions, but need to put in the time to get them all working together and looking good, then it will take an exponentially longer time for each extension we add.

How to plan

When planning our site, there are two main elements that it is essential to start with:

- a mission statement
- a list of goals

These elements help us define the direction the site is going and what the key focus of our site is. They will help us keep ourselves on track as we add to the site and pick our extensions and design.

Mission

Our mission statement describes *where* we are going with our site.

It should be a clear and succinct description of our site's reason for existence. Why does it exist and what hole does it fill? This is what we define here. It should include something measurable and socially meaningful, and cover the broadest perspective of our aspirations for the site.

It can be specific, citing figures or products, or it can be general, emphasizing a broad mission.

Some famous mission statements from real companies:

3M:

To solve unsolved problems innovatively

Mary Kay Cosmetics:

To give unlimited opportunity to women

Merck:

To preserve and improve human life

Wal-Mart:

To give ordinary folk the chance to buy the same things as rich people

Walt Disney:

To make people happy

The above mission statements may not necessarily still be the current ones for these companies, as mission statements will often change with a change in the company leadership.

These are all short, broad one-liners, but we can make ours longer if we wish. If we have a longer mission statement, it might be worth having an abbreviated version that we can use as a motto or catchphrase for our site.

Also, be careful not to just dive into our mission statement and write it in a few seconds, as it will form the basis of our site and determine the path we are going to take. We need to put a good amount of thought into the statement and our site before we start if we want the best results.

Practical—write our own mission statement

Over the course of this book, we are going to build a fully functioning subscription-based web business together. If we fully participate in the practical exercises, we will be able to walk away with our own live web business by the end of the book.

The sample web business we are going to build is going to be based on a niche in which I have a particular interest—housing in Japan. As an expatriate living in Japan, I have noticed that there is a severe lack of up to date information and assistance pertaining to housing for foreigners living in this country. So we will base our web business around selling subscriptions to information about housing and housing related topics such as gardening, repairs, renovations, and so on.

By collecting a lot of useful information about renting, or buying, in Japan, we can save other people time, the hassle, and money when they are looking for housing themselves. This is the value we will provide to our customers: time, the hassle, and money saving information about housing and related topics.

So, from this idea for the site we can come up with the following basic mission statement:

Helping foreign residents in Japan get the home they want, and not just the house that they can, by providing valuable time, money, and hassle saving information, both from our own articles and by encouraging the sharing of their own experiences and thoughts with each other.

As I mentioned earlier, mission statements can also be used to create a nice motto or catchphrase for your site. With a bit of trimming, we can get our mission statement down to:

> *Helping you get the home you want, and not just the house you can*

As we will be using this version as our catchphrase, and display it on the site for guests, I have personalized it to draw in the customers and get them thinking about my web business' product as positive for them.

Now it is your turn. Take up a piece of paper and think of the site you want to build. What are the products or services of value you are going to provide, and how are they going to benefit people? What is in it for them, and you both?

Then, if you wish, you can try to condense and personalize it into a catchphrase to show on the site.

Monetization

Before we get into our goals, it is a good time for us to put some thought into how we are going to generate an income from our site, a process called monetization. If we were just building a site for fun, for practice, or to contribute to the community, then we don't need to concern ourselves too much with this step. But if it is a web business we are building, then this is very important to our success, as the right model can make a site and the wrong one can break it.

> When building a web business, it is a good idea to cover the monetization plan before setting goals because the monetization model will usually form a significant part of our goals. We will cover monetization again in more detail later in the book.

There are several different models for generating income, the most common are:

* selling your own products
* selling someone else's products, often via affiliate links or a shop front
* advertisement-driven revenue
* subscription revenue for a service

If done correctly, any one of these is a viable income source for us. We could, for example, sell an e-book instead of having our information as articles, or we could make all our information free but put ads or affiliate links on each page that will be of interest to people living in Japan.

Even ads can be done in several different ways:

- we could swap ads with another site to give traffic to each other
- we could sell ad space for a fixed monthly fee
- we could use pay-per-click ads such as Google Adsense

Practical—decide our monetization model

For our sample site, we are planning to keep adding more and more information over time, so compiling it all into an e-book will be difficult, and we also don't have a physical product to sell or someone else's products either. This being said, advertisements or subscriptions would better suit our mission. I am personally a big fan of subscription systems because they give you ongoing repeating income which makes predicting future income much easier. Subscription systems also work well when combined with ad supported free memberships, with ads being disabled for people who purchase a subscription. This method uses people's dislike of ads as an incentive to subscribe on top of being an income generator.

Subscriptions also suit our ongoing plan of adding more information over time to the site. As the increasing information will make people want to stay longer, and thus renew subscriptions.

Housing information is not an ideal weekly or even monthly subscription though, as most people aren't going to be using the information more than once. It becomes a bit of a fine line between a one off payment and a subscription. Static information would be perfect for an e-book or a single payment to access, and regularly used information is more suited to a subscription. Because we have a blend, a longer-term subscription might be the answer, such as a yearly subscription.

A subscription isn't our only potential income source here, as advertisements could also support free content. Advertisements are best suited to a high traffic site because the number of visitors just *reading* an ad, let alone clicking on it, has been steadily reducing in recent years.

Even though there will likely be several hundred, or even thousand people looking for the information we have on offer at any given time, we aren't likely to see the sort of daily hits that would be required to make a substantial living out of advertisements. A different type of site with high demand information may be able to do so though.

By putting most of our material, except the best information, up as free to view, with ads for non-subscribers, we can also show the quality of our work and use that to build trust with potential customers, enticing them to subscribe to get our other information.

If possible, using multiple monetization models is a better option to take than relying solely on a single one. This way, if one isn't bringing in enough income, or is failing completely, you have the other to supplement it.

Now it's your turn! What kind of product or service are you offering? What kind of monetization model best suits it? Will you use only a single model, or multiple monetization models?

Goals

Now that we have our mission and have worked out how we are going to monetize our site, we need to set the specific goals for our site.

Our goals give us a detailed blueprint of exactly what we are going to provide to our users and staff. Eventually, they will give us the information we need to choose appropriate extensions for our site. Our goals should cover all the things we want our staff and customers to be able to do with the site.

Initially, it is best to adopt a brainstorming style and just put down everything we can think of that would help make the site fit the mission statement we have set. Then once we have all our ideas written down, we can start to trim those that are less relevant until we have a short, manageable list ready to go.

Practical—set our goals

For a new site, we will usually want to trim the goal list to 1-3 primary goals, and 4-6 secondary goals. Which will eventually translate into 1-3 primary extensions and 4-6 secondary ones. Why so few? First, we want to avoid making a Frankensite, but also to make it easier for us to get a professional, functioning site up and going quickly. Every extra goal we try to implement will mean more work, more styling, and more risks of failure and bugs. On top of that, customers will almost always prefer a site that does several things really well, more than a huge site that does everything poorly. So we are aiming for the former—several things done really well.

Referring back to our mission, our focus is on providing information and facilitating the sharing of information among users. So we want a combination of articles and social participation, without aiming for a full social networking site.

That leaves with a set of user goals similar to the following:

- Read articles, view videos, listen to audio
- Submit pictures/videos of their own houses/land/gardens to a public gallery
- Ask questions to each other and discuss topics

- Submit links to sites useful to other members
- Review different builders, lenders, banks, and real estate agents
- Submit their own tutorials or articles
- Submit their own story via a user blog
- View quick tips
- Comment on our articles

We also should have some goals for our staff. Even if our staff is only going to be ourselves, we need to set goals for what we wish to do with the site, so that our job running the site is as simple and efficient as possible.

So our staff goals will be:

- Submit articles which potentially contain images, video, or audio
- Restrict certain articles, and sections of other articles to subscribers only
- Upload images, video, and audio to the site for use in articles
- Approve or remove user submitted articles
- Submit useful links for display to customers
- Blog their own experiences
- Enter quick tips
- Moderate user comments and discussions

There is also a third category of goals we have. These are goals that are beneficial for the site, but not necessarily specific to customers or staff. Some of these goals relate specifically to our monetization model, or to **Search Engine Optimization** (**SEO**) to improve our placement in Google and other search engines.

- Ability to collect, moderate, and display user testimonials to build trust
- Show ads to free customers only
- Gain subscribing customers
- Convert default web page URLs to human readable links

From these lists we now need to find 1-3 main goals and 4-6 smaller ones. We can always keep the other goals to implement later, but we want a short list of features initially to maximize our new web business' potential. Also, remember that some goals could be linked, for example, staff submitting articles and users reading them, so these goals will only count as one.

For our major goals, our mission statement revolves around us passing on useful information, so our first goal will be the ability to read articles, see images, watch videos, and listen to audio. We also want to include some social aspects to keep people on the site and get them involved, so submitting their own photos and videos and having discussions will make up our other two main goals.

For our minor goals, we are intending to make a business out of our site, so we will start with allowing subscriptions combined with ads revenue from free customers.

Commenting on our articles is another good way to encourage participation. We also want the testimonials and human readable links to improve the look of our site, and our conversion rate as well. Staff submitting links should be very useful, but moderating user submitted links might be too much effort for now so we will leave only staff with that ability.

We have a lot of other good goals here, such as the evaluations of lenders and banks, or the personal blogs for users to share their stories. But we simply can't do everything without getting a Frankensite, which we definitely don't want.

So our final list looks as follows:

- Staff to submit and customers to read articles, videos, audio, and so on
- Submit pictures and videos of customer's own houses/land/gardens to a public gallery
- Ask questions to each other and discuss topics
- Grow an income from ad supported free members and subscriptions
- Staff to submit useful links for display to customers
- Customer comments on our articles
- Ability to collect, moderate, and display user testimonials to build trust
- Convert default web page URLs to human readable links

Now that we have our goal list written out, it's time to finally pick the extensions for our site.

Now it's your turn! Can you write a list of the customer and staff goals? What about general ones you need for monetization and other site benefits?

Remember that you are aiming for 1-3 primary goals, and 4-6 secondary goals.

Licenses, encryption, and commercialism

There are three very important facets of extensions that many people don't understand properly. These facets are the license under which an extension is released, if an extension is encrypted, and if so, how much is encrypted, and also the commercial nature of a product. Understanding these properly can save us a lot of headaches.

Licenses

There are two main groupings of licenses which are applied to Joomla! Extensions— open source and proprietary.

Open source

Open source licenses are so called because they generally come with a lot of freedom, and only a couple of rules. There are many different types of open source license, but the most famous and most common is the GNU General Public License, or GNU GPL license (`http://www.gnu.org/copyleft/gpl.html`). This is the license that Joomla! itself is distributed under and has the following major features:

- The code may be re-distributed without limit by those who acquire it
- The code may be modified, and even distributed after modification
- If we do modify or redistribute it, then we need to leave the original author's copyright statements in the code, giving them credit for their work
- Any code we derive from or add to GPL code must also be GPL licensed

There are more features than this, but these are the main ones.

The majority of Joomla! Extensions are also distributed with a GPL license. This is important to us as site developers mainly because it gives us the freedom to use the extension on as many sites as we want and make changes to the code.

There are other types of open source licenses, some with more freedom than the GPL and some with less.

Proprietary

At the opposite end of the spectrum are proprietary licenses, which generally contain few or no freedoms, besides being able to install and use the extension. Key features of a typical proprietary license are:

- The code cannot be re-distributed
- The code can only be installed on one web site domain for each instance of the license
- Some sections of the code may be encrypted and forbidden to alter (such as license checking code)
- Sometimes no modification is allowed at all to the code

Some proprietary licenses are more flexible than this, but many share several of these features, and possibly others.

Proprietary licenses are generally used to protect a company's income and/or intellectual property whereas open source licenses are designed to benefit the community and share knowledge while giving credit to those who share.

Which is better? It is difficult to say which is better, as it depends on who is going to use the software and how it is going to be used. For someone who just wants something to work, has little interest in making their own changes to code, or isn't going to use the code on multiple sites, then proprietary or open source will be irrelevant to their decision. However, for developers who like to make changes to their code, or have multiple web sites, the terms of the license for the extension we want should be checked out thoroughly and then decide as to whether the terms are acceptable or not.

 Originally, the official Joomla! Extension Directory stocked all extensions regardless of their license, but from mid 2009 only GNU GPL extensions will be listed. In light of this, some other extension directories have sprung up to serve non-GPL licensed extensions.

Encryption

Almost always associated with proprietary licenses (in the Joomla! environment anyway), encryption is the practice of making the source code of an extension unreadable, and unchangeable, in order to protect parts of the code from modification or copying.

It will also usually require the installation of a loader program onto our web server that enables the encrypted extension to execute.

The level of encryption on extensions varies from a single file to the entire extension, and so this should be taken into consideration when acquiring an extension, particularly if we plan to make changes to the extension.

Personally, I dislike using encrypted extensions, though I respect a developer's right to protect their work. So, I will only use them if I have no other, equal, unencrypted choice.

Commercialism

Apart from the licensing and encryption, there is a third way to divide up the extensions and this is by whether they are commercial or non-commercial, meaning do you have to pay directly to access or use them.

In the early days of Joomla!, proprietary and commercial were synonymous and there was no such thing as commercial open source extensions. Times have changed however, and there are now many commercial open source companies around, including my own company Ninja Forge (`http://ninjaforge.com`), formerly Ninjoomla, which was one of the first commercial open source companies.

There has been a long running debate over whether commercial or non commercial extensions provide better quality and/or service than the other. I believe that there is no clear-cut answer to this, as I have experienced both poor and excellent quality and service in non-commercial and commercial extensions. However, in theory at least, a commercial extension provider should be able to spend more time on the extension as they are not forced to work on another job to provide for themselves.

Using the Joomla! Extensions Directory and Google

There are currently several thousand extensions listed on the Joomla! Extensions Directory, also known as the JED (`http://extensions.joomla.org`), so it would be very difficult, if not impossible, for one person to be familiar with all of them. As a result, we will need to take our time finding just the right extensions.

Luckily, the JED is divided into categories where we can view all the extensions related to that category or topic, and it can be searched along with the Internet in general, for extensions that we want. Alternatively, we can ask other people we know who might be more knowledgeable than ourselves.

The best way to use the JED search is via the advanced search feature, which can be found at the top of the page and to the right of the search box as shown:

When searching for extensions though, I actually recommend using Google over using the built-in search on the JED if possible, as at the time of writing, the search is not as useful as it could be and tends to bring back excess results. Google searches, when limited to the JED domain, tend to bring back narrower, more accurate results.

To limit a Google search to a specific web site, first click the **Advanced Search** link on the right-hand side of the search box, as shown:

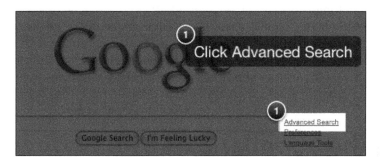

On the next page, in the **Need more tools?** section, enter extensions.joomla.org into the **Search within a site or domain** parameter as shown:

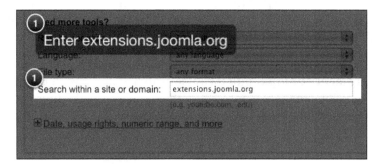

Choosing extensions from our goals

Once we have our goals worked out, and an understanding of how to search for extensions, it is time to actually start choosing the extensions we will use.

An important thing to consider as we start this process is the difference between Core and **Third Party Developer** (**3PD**) extensions.

Core extensions, are those that come with Joomla! by default, such as the content component, web links component, and contacts component. These extensions are developed and maintained by the Joomla! project team itself and generally get updated (if needed) automatically with Joomla! releases. They are mostly broadly aimed extensions that most people will use on a site, such as user management, content management, contacting the site, displaying links to other sites, and so on.

3PD extensions, on the other hand, are those made by people working separately from the Joomla! team. These extensions will generally be updated when the developer makes changes or fixes and are not reliant on Joomla! releases. 3PD extensions can augment or extend the core Joomla! Extensions by adding new features or they may introduce completely new functions and extensions, such as galleries, social networking, and so on.

When choosing extensions to meet our goals, it is often best to start with the Core extensions before looking at 3PD extensions. The reason I recommend this is because Core extensions are often more closely integrated with Joomla!, and are less likely to be affected negatively when a new version of Joomla! is released. 3PD extensions are developed separately and so a new Joomla! release may cause problems that a previous one didn't.

So, firstly we want to compare our goals to the Core extensions and see if any of them meet our needs.

 Remember that many extensions, both Core and 3PD, can be augmented by other 3PD extensions to give them more power if they don't completely fit our needs initially. The most notable of which is the content component, which can be enhanced in a seemingly unlimited number of ways by content plugins.

Once we have compared all the core components to our goals, we can start searching for 3PD extensions that meet our goals. Remember to search for ones that best fit our goals, and not just grab extensions we like, then make goals up to suit them, otherwise we will definitely end up with a Frankensite.

The first place to start would be to check the relevant categories on the JED, even before using the JED search or Google. Then, if we can't find any extensions that meet our goals, the next step would be to use the JED search or Google.

A couple of other places to look are the various featured extension pages on the JED, such as **Most Favoured**, **Editors' Pick**, **Popular Extensions**, **Top Rated**, and **Most Reviewed** because there is a good chance that other people have attempted something similar to what we are trying to do, so we may find some good extensions that match our goals there.

Let's see the process in action with our sample site.

Practical—turning goals into extensions

Looking at our goals, we can compare them to the list of the primary Core extensions like:

- Banners
- Contacts
- Content
- Mass Mail
- Media Manager
- Newsfeeds
- Polls
- Users
- Weblinks

Not all of these map to our goals, Mass Mail, for instance, isn't in our goals, nor do all our goals have a matching extension here. None of these would allow an easy method for users to upload their own images or videos to a public gallery. But some do map to our goals, and we can fill those in as shown here:

- Staff to submit and customers to read articles, videos, audio, and so on
  - ° Content to submit and read articles
  - ° Media Manager to upload images, audio, and videos
  - ° Display audio and video—None

- Submit pictures and videos of customer's own houses/land/gardens to a public gallery
  - None
- Ask questions to each other and discuss topics
  - None
- Grow an income from ad supported free members and subscriptions
  - Banners could be used for ads, but is a simple interface
  - Subscriptions — None
- Staff to submit useful links for display to customers
  - Weblinks component can fill this role
- Customer comments on our articles
  - None
- Ability to collect, moderate, and display user testimonials to build trust
  - None
- Convert default web page URLs to human readable links
  - Built-in Joomla SEF links is a simple interface, possibly not suitable

So we can fulfill one of our goals well with the Weblinks component, one can be half fulfilled with the content component, although it is missing some things. Some others are partially filled, but we may be able to find a better 3PD solution for: Banners, SEO links, and Media Manager.

Fortunately for us, I have a very good working knowledge of 3PD extensions, and my own company, Ninja Forge (`ninjaforge.com`), has produced several dozen, so we won't need to do as much searching for our sample site as others may have to.

So let's take a look at our remaining goals and what extensions we could choose from.

Display audio and video

For this goal there are two main contenders: the **AllVideos** plugin from Joomlaworks (www.joomlaworks.gr) or our own **Ninja Shadowbox** plugin. The primary difference being that AllVideos is slightly more powerful, but Ninja Shadowbox shows all the media in a pop-up like display where the screen goes dark and only the media is visible.

A weakness for Ninja Shadowbox is that while the pop-up is great for video and images, it is not so useful for an audio-only file.

A weakness for AllVideos, though, is that it doesn't do a very good job with static images. Being able to leverage the pop-ups of Ninja Shadowbox would mean we could show thumbnails of images and have the full image pop-up nicely for us.

Luckily, we don't necessarily have to choose one or the other. One of the great features of Joomla! is that we can just use both of these great plugins! We can use AllVideos for audio and video we want to be displayed on the page, and then Ninja Shadowbox for things we want to pop-up.

Ok, that is the goal decided!

Submit pictures of customers' own house to a public gallery

This next one is not so easy to fill. There are a lot of galleries available for Joomla! 1.5, and even more for Joomla! 1.0 (many of which are legacy enabled for 1.5), but very few of them allow users to upload to a public gallery. The ones I did find all require a community component called **Community Builder** to be installed first. Since we don't want to make the site into a full blown social networking site just yet, this is not desirable.

The only solution I did find is another of my company's products, **Ninja Custom Gallery**, which was created at one of my member's requests because of the lack of such a component for Joomla!.

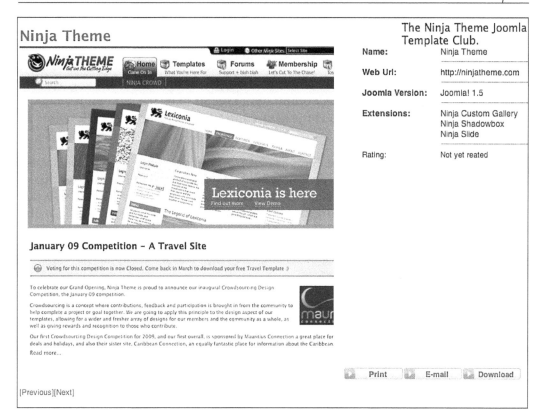

This component will allow users to submit their own images or links to videos on YouTube or Google Videos, and other users to vote for and comment on those images and videos. This gives us exactly the level of community input that we were after.

So that is another goal decided!

Ask questions to each other and discuss topics

The obvious choice for this goal is a user forum.

For Joomla! there are two main ways to get a forum onto your site. The first way is via a native extension that is installed directly into Joomla!, and the second way is by bridging an external forum application to your site, and sharing your users between Joomla! and the bridged forum.

Bridged forums are almost always significantly more powerful than the native ones because they are usually developed by teams of people and designed as a standalone forum. However, they aren't as cleanly integrated as a native forum, and they need to be styled separately.

I personally prefer native forums, because usually the focus of my sites isn't the forum itself so I don't need a full powered forum. That said though, many of the native forums are becoming quite powerful so the difference isn't great as it once was.

Looking at the three available native forums in the JED at the time of writing, we have **Agora**, **Joo!BB**, and **Simplest Forum**. Agora seems to be the most highly rated, and most used, forum of the three, but ratings don't always decide which is more suitable for us.

Looking at the demos for all three, Simplest Forum is a little too simple for my taste, and Agora seems to be a little too complex. We just want a straightforward forum with a few features in it. The developer of the remaining forum, Joo!BB, says that the forum is still only in Beta and warns not to use it on production sites, however, many reviews seem to say that it is really quite stable despite the developer's warning.

I think we will go with Joo!BB for our forum, with Agora as a backup, if it doesn't turn out to work for us.

Grow an income from ad-supported free members and subscriptions

This is one of the most important goals for us to get right, because if we do it wrong then we could have some significant issues with income for our web business.

Going to the **Paid Access and Content** category on the JED, we are presented with a list of subscription management systems among others.

After looking at the options available, our main contenders here are **AEC** and **JoomSuite Member**. AEC is listed as being only Joomla! 1.0 compatible, but if we check the web site, the development versions work on Joomla! 1.5 if Legacy mode is enabled. Also, a native version is coming soon. AEC has a lot of positive reviews and votes and appears to be quite a mature and solid extension, all bonuses in its favor. It also has a substantial array of features and is very flexible as a result.

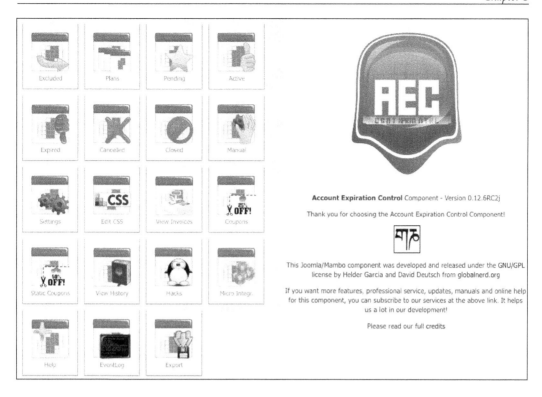

JoomSuite Member is also very appealing looking component, seeming to be both powerful and flexible. But, it has some disadvantages from my personal point of view. It has a proprietary license, and some portions of the code are encrypted. This means that should anything happen to the developing company then we could lose our subscription component if anything goes wrong. Also, since we can't edit all of the code, we are limited in what we can do with it.

For most people, this will likely never cause a problem, so for them JoomSuite Member definitely appears to be a great component. But I prefer to use open source whenever possible because I can see and change the components if I need to, and the survival of my company is not reliant on the survival of another company.

So even though it means we need to use Legacy Mode, it looks like AEC will be our subscription manager.

As for the ads, Google ads are definitely the easiest to start with, and as our site traffic grows we can expand later to purchased or affiliate ads. So looking in the Google ads category on the JED, there are close to three dozen different Google ad modules and plugins available. Seeing as Google ads aren't really that complex, all of the modules and plugins are most likely going to be very similar in operation, so let's just pick one of the top rated ones and get it over with.

The **Clicksafe special edition** from **Joomlaspan** looks like a good choice as a module for us, as not clicking our own ads sounds good to me. Also, the **MultiAds** plugin also looks like it will enable us to put ads into our content as well.

However, we also want to hide our ads from paying subscribers and some of our content as well. How can we do this?

There are several plugins and modules around that allow people to hide and show content based on a person's access group, as can be found in the **Content Restriction** or **Group Access** categories on the JED.

But again, we will go with some of my company's own products — The **Ninja Access** plugin and module, simply because I know the code better than some of the other available options which are all just as good.

Customer comments on our articles

The comments category on the JED contains a large array of comment systems, far too many for us to check them all, but thankfully we can just look at the top rated ones to find some very nice comment systems.

JoomlaComment appears to be a good choice, but it is only Joomla! 1.0 compatible. However, it does support Legacy Mode. **Jxtended Comments** is also a great looking extension. There is also **Jom Comment** and **Chrono Comment** that appear to meet our needs.

As we will already be using Legacy Mode for our subscription system, AEC, it doesn't matter too much if we have another extension using it, as long as both of them eventually become Joomla 1.5 native. On the web site for JoomlaComment, they say that they are working on a native Joomla 1.5 version, so hopefully it won't be too far away.

Jxtended Comments and Jom Comment both look very good, but both are very advanced with a lot more features than we need. We aren't expecting a massive amount of comments on our articles, as they will mostly be fact based, and thus there won't be much to comment on, so equipping our comment system with all of these features will just be a waste.

Lastly we have Chrono Comment, which at first was my preferred choice. However, after inspecting their license there are a few clauses that make it potentially difficult to use in the future.

So it looks like we will be going with JoomlaComment shown as follows:

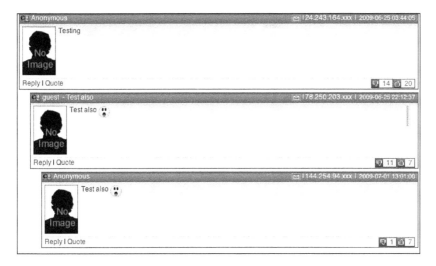

Ability to collect, moderate, and display user testimonials

Many marketers feel that testimonials are essential, or at least very important, to the success of a web business, as they provide honest, and usually positive, feedback from your existing customers to your potential customers. This sort of feedback may be crucial in convincing people who are unsure about your product or service that it will provide them with good value for money.

Looking on the JED, the only testimonial extension at the time of writing is **Ninjamonials**, which thankfully does everything we need. It has a frontend interface for collecting and displaying testimonials from and to customers, and it also has an administration interface for managing them. There is also a module allowing us to display random testimonials on different pages of the site. It should do nicely.

Convert default web page URLs to human-readable links

While the default Joomla! SEF links option works, technically speaking, it doesn't really do much to improve the readability of the links, so we want to look for a more advanced 3PD solution.

Looking in the **SEO** and **Metadata** category on the JED, there looks to be one clear leader for Joomla! 1.5, and that is **sh404SEF**. It is an editor's pick and has more, and higher, votes and reviews than any other extensions in the category.

So our last one was pretty easy as well!

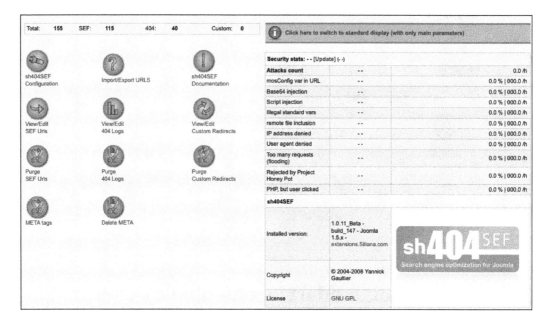

Now it's your turn! Take your goals and start to look for extensions that will help you fill them. Remember to start with the Core extensions and then move onto 3PD extensions, searching via the JED or Google. Once you have done this, it is time to add some essential extensions to your site.

Essential extensions

Apart from the extensions that we include for our goals, there are also some extensions that we should install into our site. I consider these extensions essential because they provide such strong benefits to a site administrator that leaving them out puts us at a disadvantage, or makes our work harder than it should be.

This list is not complete, nor are these the only extensions that could be considered essential, but they are general enough that most people will want most or all of them on their sites.

The extensions are described in the sections that follow.

NinjaXplorer

NinjaXplorer (`http://ninjaforge.com`) gives us a stable and useful file management system within our Joomla! administrator interface. It is especially useful for uploading small groups of files, and serves as an alternative to FTP.

We can also make edits to files, allowing us to make small changes to files without having to download, edit, and upload them again. It is also possible to change the file permissions on files, copy them, rename them, move them, and more.

Furthermore, unlike the Media Manager, NinjaXplorer is not limited to only the media directory.

JoomlaPack

I consider **JoomlaPack** (`http://www.joomlapack.net`) essential because it is one of the best backup methods around for Joomla!, enabling us to completely restore a site, and every file in it from nothing.

It is almost assured that at some point in the life of our site, we are going to have our site destroyed by matters outside our hands. It could be our hosting company, it could be a malicious hacker, it could be a natural disaster, it could be one of our staff, or it could even be a mistake we made by ourselves. Anyone who doesn't make regular backups of their site is playing a game of *Russian roulette* with its future. If we are making an income from our site, it is especially important for us to keep the site safe.

It is also useful if we want to move, or duplicate a site since we can just make a copy and install it, database and all, onto a new domain or server. Thereby, we save quite a bit of time, if we want to produce a site similar to an existing one.

JCE

The default WYSIWYG (What You See Is What You Get) editor for Joomla is quite good, but there are a number of more fully featured 3PD editors available. My personal favorite is **Joomla Content Editor**, or JCE (`http://www.joomlacontenteditor.net`).

The reason why many consider a 3PD WYSIWYG editor like JCE as essential is because they can dramatically reduce the time it takes to write articles, especially if we usually include a lot of formatting in them. JCE also has built-in user controls, so we can control exactly what features we want our editors or other users to have. For example, if we don't want them to be able to upload images, then we can turn off the image button, or only allow them to upload images into a certain directory and so on.

EasySQL

Sometimes we need to make changes to our database, analyze some data, extract records, or simply change something quickly and easily.

EasySQL (`http://lurm.net/?other/easysql`) is an extension that allows us to do small changes in a much faster time than a full blown database tool like phpMyAdmin.

It is not as powerful for beginners though, as the real power comes when we can write our own database interaction queries using the programming language SQL. However, it can still be useful for quick changes.

While we could probably live without having EasySQL installed, it makes things a lot easier if it is when it comes time to make changes to our database.

The above-mentioned extensions, with the exception of a WYSIWYG editor, only have an administrator interface so they don't need to be styled. Thus it is relatively safe to install them without needing to fear becoming a Frankensite. Even the WYSIWYG, JCE, has standard buttons that are simple enough to match any site.

Summary

There was quite a lot of reading and thinking in this chapter, but we should now be well on the way to finishing our planning and being prepared to start on our site.

After discussing why it's important to plan, we wrote out our mission statement, decided how we would monetize our site, and then wrote our list of goals. We then turned those goals into extensions, starting with Core extensions and moving out to 3PDs, and then to the essential extensions that every site should have.

During it all we set the mission, monetization model, goals, and extensions for our sample site and it is ready to go!

However, before we get to building our site, we need to take a look at the technologies that make up Joomla: primarily HTML, PHP, CSS, and JavaScript. Once we have a basic understanding of these we will be finally ready to start setting up our site.

4
Installing and Configuring Extensions

Now that we have our mission, our goals, our list of extensions, and an understanding of how it all fits together, it is time to start putting it all together and assemble our site. Since we already know how to install a basic Joomla! site, we will start with our site configuration and then move into our extensions.

This chapter will primarily be practical with us in setting up the extensions on our sample site and walking through the process for selecting them. But the same process can be applied to any of our own sites.

We will cover:

- Configuring Joomla! — Core extensions and configuration
- Configuring content sections and categories — clearing sample content and creating new sections and categories
- Configuring extensions — work through our main extensions for our site

Configuring Joomla!

When installing Joomla!, we have the option of installing it with a minimum configuration or to add sample data. It is usually better to start with the sample data and then remove, or change the things we don't want or need, as the minimum configuration leaves many people wondering where to start with their site. At least with the sample data we will have a working site right from the start and be able to visualize the changes we want to make.

Core extensions

The first thing we will do with our site is remove or disable any Core extensions that we don't need on our site. This is done mainly to reduce clutter and make the site easier for us to work with. It may also potentially improve the performance of our site, but probably not enough to be noticeable.

Some Core extensions can be removed without negative effects, but others are important to the running of Joomla! or are intertwined with Core tables and so we are only able to disable these extensions, not uninstall them.

Components

To begin, click the **Extensions | Install/Uninstall** menu item. Then select **Components** from the **Extension Manager** menu as shown:

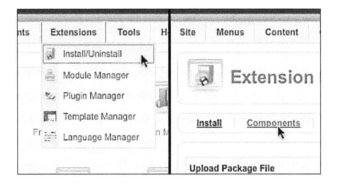

Next, we need to identify any Core components that we want to uninstall or if we can't uninstall them, at least disable them. Only four Core components can be removed, but most components can be disabled, if we aren't going to use them.

The only four Core components that can be uninstalled are:

- Banners
- Newsfeeds
- Polls
- Weblinks

Of these, the one we definitely don't need in our sample site is **Newsfeeds** so we can uninstall this one. We also don't have any plans for **Polls**, but it might be useful in the future as running polls to get user feedback is often a useful idea, but as we don't need it right now, let's disable it. We may want to use **Banners** for our advertising, so we will leave it for now, and we might also want to use **Weblinks** so we will leave it in place too.

 It's easy to identify core modules and components that we can't uninstall because they will be grayed out and unselectable. All components have the **Enabled** field clickable though, and we can use this to enable and disable them. Modules and plugins lack this field.

So, of the four removable Core components, we will remove one, disable one, and leave two enabled.

Of the remaining Core components, the only other one we don't need is **Mass Mail**, because, as we will see later, using a hosted email newsletter is a much better alternative to the built-in Mass Mail component. We will disable this also.

Modules

Now click **Modules** in the **Extension Manager** menu. There are 34 core modules in total, 17 of which we can remove if we wish. Rather than list them all, we will just look at the ones we are going to remove or disable and why.

- `mod_newsflash`—our site isn't a news site and we have no plans to display newsflash like snippets so we can uninstall this one

- `mod_poll`—like the component, we may use this in the future so we will just disable it for now

- `mod_random_image`—there is no real use for us to display random images so we can uninstall it

- `mod_stats`—not needed at all, especially since we removed the component which supports it so can be uninstalled

- `mod_wrapper`—we have no need to bring content in from other sites in a module so we can remove this one

- `mod_archive`—we can't uninstall this one, but we don't need it so let's disable it

The rest we need or may need so we can leave them as is.

Plugins

Since there are less plugins, and we won't usually spend a lot of time working with them, it isn't as useful to remove unused plugins. Also, plugins can't be disabled from the extension manager, they can only be disabled from within the the plugin manager. But we will take a look in the extension manager just to be consistent.

Plugins are divided into their different types. It's easy to see what type a plugin is, as the type name is usually written before the plugin name. Here are two that we don't need:

- Authentication—Gmail—we don't need this at all, so we can uninstall it
- Search—Newsfeeds—we removed all our other Newsfeeds extensions so we can uninstall this one as well

Global Configuration

Now that we have cleaned out unneeded core extensions, let's look at our site configuration. Click the **Site | Global Configuration** menu item.

There are three main areas to the **Global Configuration** screen: **Site**, **System**, and **Server**. Initially we will only change a few settings, but we will return later to change other settings we need.

Under **Site | Global Configuration | Site Settings**, let's set the site name (if we didn't during installation). It's useful to have a site name that includes a few keywords to describe our site. This helps search engines like Google and Yahoo to index our site more correctly. We are going to use: **Your Japanese House – How to buy or rent a house in Japan**. This has a few of our most important key words in it and is still useful to visitors.

Let's also set the **Global Site Meta Description** to something useful that describes our site. While not essential to our site, having a good description may slightly improve our search engine ranking. Generally, this will be under 200 characters, or around 20 words, and should be quite concise. We will go with: **Your Japanese House.com can help foreigners, gaijin, to buy or rent their own house, apartment, or investment property in Japan**.

Next we will set the **Global Site Meta Keywords**. Similar to the description, the keywords are not essential but can potentially improve our search engine ranking so they are worth filling in. The best length is around 10-15 keywords. We will use the following keywords for Your Japanese House: **house japan, japanese house, buy japanese house, rent japanese house, buy house japan, rent in japan, buy land japan**.

This should just about do us for now for the site configuration. Time to install and configure our extensions!

Configuring content sections and categories

Now that Joomla! is configured, but before we configure our extensions, we should first configure the sections and categories that we need for our content. Our site is going to be primarily based around passing on information to our visitors, so how we organize our content is important.

Clearing out the sample content

Before we create any new sections, categories, or content, we should remove all the existing sample content items, sections, and categories.

We need to start with the content first. Click **Content | Article Manager**. Select all the content items by clicking the checkbox in the table header, then click **Trash**. If we have any articles remaining, such as when we have multiple pages of articles, we should repeat this process until we have removed them all.

When we click the **Trash** button, the articles are not yet truly deleted, and they have simply been moved to the **Article Trash** area. Until we completely delete these articles, we won't be able to remove the sections and categories that we don't need.

Click **Content | Article Trash** and then delete all our sample content. From here we can go to **Content | Category Manager** and **Content | Section Manager** and remove our sample categories and sections.

Creating sections

Lucky for us, we have a precise mission and goal to help us narrow down what sort of content is going onto the site. It is easy to go overboard and think "I can put up categories for everything and everyone will want to come and read it!", but the fact is, just like with our extensions, less pages of more focused useful information will have a stronger appeal than more pages of unspecific non-useful information.

Our mission is to provide information on buying and renting houses in Japan, and so these two topics should be the focus of our material and make up our two main categories. There will also be some material that fits both categories without being specific to either, or fits neither category (such as connecting utilities or dealing with removal companies). Hence, we will also need a general section to hold this information. This gives us three sections to start our site with:

- Buying in Japan
- Renting in Japan
- General Housing Matters

Creating categories

Now we need to fill out some categories for these three sections. Remember that as we add content to the site we may think of more categories, or we may remove or combine some that we have no material for so this list is probably not permanent.

After some brainstorming, I came up with the following categories:

Buying in Japan

- Financing
- New Homes
- Used Homes
- Investment Properties
- Inspections
- Check Lists
- Insurance
- Government Matters
- Buying General

Renting in Japan

- Finding and Choosing
- Money Matters
- Check Lists
- Moving In/Out
- Government Matters

General Housing Matters

- Utilities
- Moving House
- Government Matters

Buying in Japan has quite a lot of sections, and the General section only has three, but this is fine. All that matters is that there is enough to cover the topics our content will be about, but not too many that we can't actually get any content into them.

 It is better to have fewer categories displayed than to have empty categories. So if we can't put articles into all our categories before launch they should not be created. We should not publish any empty categories (and sections) until we have articles for them.

Configuring extensions

When configuring our extensions, it is important to make sure that we are setting them up to align with the goals and mission we set earlier. Keeping notes on these handy will make configuring our extensions quicker and easier.

AEC

AEC is likely to be the biggest, and most difficult, extension to configure on our site. The wide array of settings and configurations required can be daunting to a beginner, or even someone experienced with it. Thankfully, there are only a few settings that most people will need to use on their sites.

To download AEC, we need to go to http://valanx.org/.

The first thing we need to do is go to **Extensions | Plugin Manager** and activate the **System | Legacy** plugin. As AEC is still only native to Joomla! 1.0, we need to activate this plugin to get it to work on Joomla! 1.5.

Next we need to install the AEC component and the two plugins that come with it.

Before we configure AEC, we need to make some decisions. First, what sort of **subscription plans** are we going to offer, and secondly, what **payment gateways** are we going to use.

Subscription plans

One of the most important parts of our configuration, and one that can make or break a subscription site, is how we setup our plans.

How much will we charge, and for how long will we offer our subscriptions?

Generally, how much to charge can be determined by looking at things from the customer's perspective. Ask yourself how much is this worth to me as a customer? Something that will save a customer a lot of time or money, or make them a lot of money, will be worth more than something that only saves or makes them a little.

Also, we need to consider the financial situation of the customers we want to attract. Are we selling investment advice to millionaires or tips on living in a box to the homeless?

Finally, consider the number of customers we might be able to sell to. We can often, but not always, make more income by charging less per item and selling more, than charging more and selling fewer items. This does sometimes work in reverse though, as charging too little may make our product seem worthless or make us look desperate.

There will always be a sweet spot balance between price per item and number of items we sell, to produce the maximum profit for our site. Finding it may take some tweaking of our subscription plans over a few months.

As for the duration of a subscription, that depends mainly on the frequency of our updates and the relevance of our information or service to their daily lives. For example, if it's something they will use daily or weekly, then we can have a weekly or monthly subscription. However, if we only update once a month or our information is something used occasionally, then a longer period may be in order.

The purpose of picking the duration is to make it the right length that people will want to keep their subscription to our site. If it is too short, then people will cancel their subscriptions, if it is too long then we are losing money on renewals.

For our sample site, Your Japanese House, we probably don't have the best product for a short-term subscription as not many people will be buying houses very often. However, it may be worth someone who is in the market for a house to keep their access for a few months until they make their purchase or get their lease.

On a plus side, however, since our information could save people hundreds or even thousands of dollars in both saved time and money, we can charge a reasonable price for our subscriptions.

Unfortunately, we probably won't get a lot of repeat subscribers, except for professional investors, unless we expand our information into something that is useful regularly. Since our information will change over time, it is still preferable to have a subscription model over a one off book sale for example, as there is a chance for repeat subscriptions however slim they may be.

So regarding the durations, having a 6-month plan and a 12-month plan may work best for us. It should also be noted that it is often worth having a lifetime plan with a suitably high price (usually 2 to 3 years equivalent) as a way to bring in occasional large payments.

Since we are talking about potentially hundreds of dollars in savings, (although it will be in Japanese Yen) a one year subscription will easily be worth around $60. Then, rather than being half the price of the yearly subscription, we will set the 6-month subscription at about 60-65% of the yearly price (in this case $40). This provides more incentive to go for the one year plan as it provides better value for money. For our lifetime subscriptions, a little over 2 years price, at $150 seems high enough to be a payment worth receiving, but not so expensive as to be unreasonable to a customer.

It is also worth considering if we are going to set up our plans as auto-renewing (and thus automatically acquiring money from our customers) or one off payments that are left up to the user to renew. Generally, one off payments work better for long-term, higher priced subscriptions, and recurring for lower priced monthly or weekly subscriptions.

This is because a sudden $60 or higher payment disappearing from their account a year after they signed up will often result in us receiving an angry mail from the customer demanding their money back. However, a monthly or weekly subscription becomes something they are used to seeing regularly.

We need to think about this because it will affect our site configuration later, especially with our subscription manager AEC. As we are using longer duration, higher priced subscriptions, we will go with non-recurring payments.

So now that we have three plans decided for our customers, it's time to look at payment gateways.

Payment gateways

Because most of us aren't a bank, and don't have one handy, we need a way to collect and send money over the Internet. Thankfully, we aren't alone, and entire industries have risen up to service this need for sending and receiving money over the Internet.

Services that allow web site owners to accept payments from their site are usually referred to as payment gateways.

There are dozens, perhaps hundreds, of different payment gateways around the world, but two of the biggest and most common are Paypal, and 2CO. Many banks also offer credit card services to allow us to accept credit cards on our site.

2CO is very widely available in different countries around the world, but has a very strict process for application requiring us to have various pages on our site and provide various documents to verify our personal and business identity.

Paypal is not as widely available globally as 2CO, but has a much simpler and smoother application process. Usually, they require only that we register an account, and then register either a credit card or bank account with them to allow we to transfer funds and confirm our identity.

For our sample site, we will use PayPal as it is the most convenient and includes Japan (where the bulk of our expected customers will be from). PayPal can be found at http://www.paypal.com.

General Configuration

To get to the AEC **General Configuration** page, click the menu item **Components | AEC Subscription Manager | Settings** and we will be presented with a series of tabs, the first of which, **Global**, contains our **General Configuration** page.

There are some settings we need to adjust here, and some we don't. It is this time that we will need our goals list nearby to confirm if our settings match our goals or not. Since there are detailed tooltips for the items, we will only cover those that we need to change or that we want to confirm. The rest can be left at their default values or changed to suit our site if needed.

- **Require Subscription**: Subscriptions are a major part of our monetization model, so we will set this to **Yes**.
- **No Emails**: Make sure this is set to **No**. Because it is a double negative, it's difficult to realize at first, but setting this to no will mean that we *do* send out AEC emails, which may be needed to help keep customers informed of their account status.
- **No Joomla Emails**: We are only allowing people with a valid subscription to sign in, so there is no need to send confirmation emails, which are mainly an anti-spamming tool. Because the subscription won't activate until it is paid, if they pay for a subscription each time then spammers are welcome to join if they want.
- **Activated Gateways**: For this, we are going to select PayPal and *not* PayPal Subscription, because we don't need recurring subscriptions. After we save this screen once (not yet), we will see tabs appear to configure PayPal and any other payment gateways we select.

PayPal requires slightly different commands to be sent to it depending on whether you want to make a one off payment or a recurring payment. This is why there are two sets of PayPal configuration, one for one-time payments and one for recurring payments.

- **Entry Plan**: Set this to **None**. We want to only allow people who have paid for a subscription to access the site. If entry plan is set to anything except none then whenever someone registers, they can skip the payment or cancel at PayPal, and then revisit our site and AEC will automatically give them the default plan specified here. We don't want a default plan, we want people in or out of our paid plan, so we will set it to **None**.

- **Plans First**: Set this to **Yes**. As stated many times, we will require people to pay for a membership, so if we make sure that they have decided to pay before they sign up, then we don't get people creating accounts with no intention of subscribing.

- **Integrate Registration**: Set this to **Yes** for the same reasons as above.

- **Enable Coupons**: We can set this to yes or no depending on whether we want to use them or not. We might use them at some point, so let's enable them for now.

- **Skip Confirmation**: It is alleged that a site will lose 5-25% of their potential customers from each unnecessary click during registration, so we want to reduce the number of page loads and clicks as much as possible. Therefore, we will set this to **Yes**.

There are other parameters on this tab which we can use to alter the settings of to suit our site, but these are the most important ones.

Customization

Under the **Customize** tab, we have a lot of parameters that enable us to replace the default AEC pages, currency symbol, and so on. Right now, we don't need to change any of these for our site but as we develop it, we may wish to come back and add some new pages for the thanks page or add a terms of service for example.

Micro Integrations

Micro Integrations are small scripts that run when a customer subscribes, or un-subscribes, from our site. They usually perform some task for a different extension, such as adding a number of downloads to a download manager, sending an email, creating a directory, or setting access levels. These are very useful if we are using a large variety of complex extensions. But, as we are aiming for a clean simple site upfront, we won't use any of these except the defaults for now.

Authentication plugins

Under the **Authentication** tab, we find two multiselect boxes. But the most important part about this tab is the tooltip for the two boxes. It tells us that we need to make sure that the only Authentication plugin we have active is the AEC one, and that we should then use these boxes to select which other authentication plugins to use.

So at this point, we will save our configuration using the **Save** button, and then click **Extensions | Plugin Manager**. Next, let's ensure that all the **Authentication – xxxx** plugins are disabled except **Authentication – AEC**. Once this is done, we can go back to **Components | AEC Subscription Manager | Settings**. Now, our **PayPal** tab should have appeared for us.

PayPal

We now have our **PayPal** configuration tab available to us and we can configure our payment gateway. The fields that are important to us are:

- **Business ID**: We enter the email that we have configured at `paypal.com`.
- **Test Mode?**: Test mode is used if we have set up accounts at the PayPal Sandbox, and wish to test our site without having to spend real money. If we were going to put complicated plans, many plans, or different vouchers, this may be worth doing to help with our testing. Be aware that setting up the test accounts can take a lot of time that could be more easily tested with two PayPal accounts and just refunding the money. We will go with **No** here.
- **Currency Selection**: Our site is going to be targeted at people living in Japan, so we will choose **Japanese Yen** here.
- **Language**: Even though our currency is going to be Yen, our visitors are mainly going to be English speakers, as our content will mostly be English and is aimed at foreigners in Japan, so we will make sure we have the language set to **English**.

The rest of the parameters are for the appearance of the page at the PayPal site and on our own site, so we can set these however we like.

Creating subscription plans

Now that we have done our initial configuration of AEC and decided on our plans and payment processor, we can now actually create the plans.

Click on **Components | AEC Subscription Manager | Plans**, then click the **New** button in the top right-hand corner to start creating our plan.

There are several tabs here, but the **Restrictions, Trial Period, Relations,** and **Micro Integrations** aren't needed for our trial site so we can ignore them. **Plan Text** will be useful for us later when we are styling our site, but isn't needed right now.

Let's start with the **Plan** tab. The parameters we need to change, and check, are:

- **Name**: Put in the name of this plan. This will be our 6-month plan, but that makes for a boring name. Let's call it the *Basic Plan*.
- **Published**: Yes.
- **Visible**: Yes — this tells AEC, if the plan is to be listed on the plans page or hidden, which makes it useful for things like an automatic plan or a fallback plan (when their plan expires).
- **Enable usergroup**: Yes — we want our new members to be given a registered level account. This probably isn't needed as they will be registered, by default, by Joomla!, but better safe than sorry.
- **Add user to Group**: Registered — make sure our new members get put into the right group.
- **Make Active**: Yes — we don't want to be manually activating members.
- **Primary**: Yes — we only have one subscription per user.
- **Override Activation**: Yes — there is no need for the Joomla! default activation process with paid plans.
- **Override Registration Email**: Yes — there is no need for this with paid registrations.
- **Plan Fallback**: No Plan — if a member's account expires, we want them to not be able to log in again until they renew their subscription.
- **Free**: No.
- **Regular Rate**: 3900 — remember we are dealing with Yen and 100 Yen is equivalent to around 1 US Dollar.
- **Lifetime**: No.
- **Period**: 6.
- **Period Unit**: Months.

Now click the **Processors** tab and check the **Active** checkbox to enable our Basic Plan to use our PayPal payment gateway.

With that we are done! Our new plan is ready to go. Now we can go through and repeat the process for our other 2 plans: Home Buyer/1 Year/5900 Yen, Professional/Lifetime/14,900 yen.

Once we have finished those, we are done for now with the AEC configuration.

Joo!BB

Now that we have configured our subscriptions, it is time to configure our forum that is using Joo!BB, which we can pick up at `http://www.joobb.org/`.

When configuring a forum, sometimes called a bulletin board, there are two main areas that we need to configure. The first is the actual configuration of the forum as a whole, and the second is the structure of the forum, that is what different boards and forums will we set up for people to chat in.

Configuring boards

The first thing we should decide is what boards we will create in our forum. To do this we need to think about the sort of things that our visitors are going to want to talk about.

When deciding on boards for a new forum, especially for a new site, it is important to keep the number of boards and sub-boards low initially for a couple of reasons. First of all, it is much easier to add new boards and create new topics of discussion, than it is to remove them. Secondly, a new site will usually only have low traffic, so the more boards we have, the more empty our forum will look. Since many people will judge the quality of our site by how busy the community seems, we want to avoid having empty forums.

Our site is focused around Japanese housing related matters, in particular buying and renting houses in Japan. This opens us up to a huge number of potential boards with topics ranging from getting a home loan, to gardening, to disaster preparation, and more. However, as we said above, we want to keep it relatively compact initially to make our site seem busier, so we will start with only 4 or 5 forums and build up from there as our site grows.

The two main topics for our site content will be buying and renting houses, so they should be our first two boards. Then, we can have a general topics board for non-housing related discussions and finally, a general house matters board giving us:

- Buying in Japan
- Renting in Japan
- General Housing Matters
- General Topics

Now let's create them. Click on **Components | Joo!BB,** and we will be presented with a screen containing a lot of buttons that link to different parts of the forum configuration as shown here:

From this screen, click the **Board** button. We should now see a screen like the one shown here:

Before we create our boards, Joo!BB requires us to have categories to put our boards into. This is a good idea as it allows us to organize a large board into manageable parts. We only have a small board though, so we will only need one category.

Click the **Categories** menu item on the **Forum Manager** menu. On the next screen we will click on the **Test Category** and rename it to **General Forum**. Then, click **Forums** in the menu.

Now let's delete the **Test Board** and create a new one. In the **Forum Manager – Add** screen we have two main groups of parameters, **Forum Details** on the left and **Forum Permissions** on the right. **Forum Information** at the bottom is not for parameters, but contains the current statistics of the forum.

The parameters we want to set on the left-hand side are:

- **Name**: Buying a House in Japan — one of our forum names we decided before
- **Description**: Discuss matters related to buying houses in Japan
- **Category**: General Forum
- **Enabled**: Yes
- **Locked**: No
- **New Posts Time**: 600

On the right-hand side, we need to think about things a little more. We are going to restrict registration to only paying members, but initially we want to get as much activity on our forums as possible so we will allow even the non-registered people to post and reply to threads. So, we need to change these from *Registered* to *All*. But we can leave everything else as it is for now.

Once our membership has grown and our forum is busy, we can deny access to some of the more important forums to non-registered visitors, thus, motivating them to sign up.

Repeat this for our other three forums and we will have finished configuring our boards.

Overall Configuration of Joo!BB

Click either the Joo!BB arrow in the top-right, or click **Components | Joo!BB** to go back to the main Joo!BB page. Next, click on **Configuration** and we will be taken to the **Configuration Manager** screen as shown:

Click on the link **Joo!BB Standard Configuration**. The next page has a long list of configuration options split into two columns. Let's go through the options we need to change or confirm:

Configuration details

The parameters we need look into are:

- **Name**: We don't need to change this unless we want to as it is just the name for these configuration details
- **Time Zone**: UTC +9:00 — we are on Japan time
- **Board Name**: Your Japanese House — Forum

Board settings

- **Description**: The YJH Forum is the place to discuss anything related to buying or renting a house in Japan
- **Keywords**: house japan, japanese house, buy japanese house, rent japanese house, buy house japan, rent in japan, buy land japan, japanese garden, garden japan — the same as for our site
- **Account Activation**: None — AEC will handle all account related details

There are others that we may want to adjust in the future, but the defaults are fine for now.

Latest post settings

We can leave these as default for now.

Feed settings

We can leave these as default for now, but we should fill them out with something appropriate before we go live.

Attachments

- **Enable Attachments**: Yes

View settings

- **Show Statistics**: No — we want to hide our statistics initially while the forum is small to hide the fact that it is not too busy yet
- **Show Who's Online**: No — as above, we want this off to hide the fact that we don't have much activity yet

View footer settings

- **Show Logout**: No — AEC is to handle this
- **Show Login**: No — as above
- **Show Register**: No — as above

Registration User Settings Defaults

- Time Zone: UTC +9:00 – We are on Japan time

Avatar settings

- **Enable Avatars**: Yes
- **Image Resize**: Yes — we don't want massive avatars being uploaded
- **Image Resize Quality**: 100 — keep images at the quality in which they were uploaded
- **Avatar Maximum Width**: 100 — lets set our avatars to be 100x100px
- **Avatar Maximum Height**: 100
- **Avatar Maximum File Size**: 8192 — 8k is fine for avatar images

Captcha settings

We can leave these as default for now.

We have now finished configuring Joo!BB and have also created a few boards to start our forum off. Our forum should be pretty much ready to go now.

!JoomlaComment

!JoomlaComment, available at `http://compojoom.com/`, consists of a combination of a component and a content plugin, but the plugin is installed automatically with the component so we only need to install one file.

Once installed we need to do a bit of configuring, but a lot less than our forum or subscription manager. To access the configuration click **Components | !JoomlaComment | Content Settings**.

The **Content Settings** screen, which should now load, will have four tabs at the top of the page. We will look at each tab separately.

General

Surprisingly, these can all be left as default. There is nothing we wish to do that is out of the ordinary as far as the basic operation of our comments goes.

Security

Most of these will be left as default, but we will change a few and check most of the others.

- **Only registered:** No — we want guests to be able to comment to build up the appearance of activity on our site and get people involved enough that they register.

- **Autopublish comments:** Yes — this is a personal preference and may be changed in the future, but generally our visitors should be responsible adults and our information will mostly be factual and not just opinion, so we aren't likely to attract inappropriate comments. If our site was, for example, a political or news site where many people may post aggressive or offensive comments, we would probably turn this on.

- **Notify moderators:** Yes — this is another personal preference, but we aren't expecting our site to have a huge amount of traffic so allowing email notifications shouldn't put too much of a strain on our inbox. If our site was expected to become very popular, then we may want to turn this off and batch moderate comments once a day or so.

- **Moderator groups:** S Administrator — we don't have a large staff, so initially the emails should all come to us.

- **Enable users notification:** Yes.

- **Enable comment Feed (RSS):** Yes — this probably won't be of much use, but it won't hurt to have it.

- **Post max length**: 5000 — comments on our articles, being factual in nature, are likely to be longer than on a news site or the like. Visitors may wish to share their own experience, add supporting facts, or dispute the information in the article. For these reasons let's give them more space for their comments.

- **Captcha Enabled** (recommended): Yes — we need capture to stop un-registered visitors, that could be spam bots, from spamming our site.

- **Captcha Usertypes**: Unregistered — we only need to use captcha for our unregistered visitors. Registered visitors have paid money and so are unlikely to be spam bots.

- **Website URL only for registered**: Yes — this can be a benefit for our paying users, the ability to add their URL to their comments.

- **Censorship | Enable**: Yes — this censorship is really controlling the language used and not true censorship. Because we are giving a fair bit of freedom to our commenting visitors, and our audience should be family friendly, we may want to put some light level censorship on and filter out any inappropriate words.

- **Censored Words**: We will add some words here that we don't wish to see used in our comments. All words should be comma-separated and if we provide two words, make sure they are separated by an equals = sign, then the any occurrences of the first word will be replaced by the second one, but if we only list one word inside the comma, that word will simply be removed entirely.

- **Usertypes**: Unregistered, Registered — we probably only need the filter on unregistered users, but better safe than sorry.

Posting

There are only two that we need to change here. The rest are fine with the default values.

- **Enable Profiles**: No — we don't use Community Builder, so no need to link to it

- **Enable Avatars**: No — as above. (note that this applies to community builder avatars only)

Layout

We don't need to change any of the layout settings yet, but we will come back here later when we are working on the styling for our site. We can save our changes and we are done with !JoomlaComment.

Ninja Custom Gallery

We are using Ninja Custom Gallery to allow our members to upload images or videos of their own homes, and then allow them to comment on the images and rate them.

Ninja Custom Gallery is a little more complex than a standard gallery because on top of image and videos, it also allows the site administrator to create custom fields associated with the images and the users to fill in the fields when submitting an image.

The fields themselves get organized into categories which get assigned to a gallery. This allows galleries to share similar lists of custom items without having to create the same items over and over.

Categories

To start with, we need to think about the types of images and videos we want people to put up, and then we can create galleries and categories to accommodate these. Ideally, we want images of houses, apartments, and possibly gardens and interiors. That gives us a decent range of images to collect for our users to look at and comment on.

Houses and apartments will work best as separate galleries, but they will both have the same custom fields associated with them. So we can make a single category of buildings to handle them. Gardens and interiors are quite different, so we will have separate categories and galleries for each of them.

So our categories are:

- Buildings
- Gardens
- Interiors

To create a category, click **Components | Ninja Custom Gallery | Categories**, then click the **New** button on the top-right-hand corner.

Categories are pretty easy to set up; we just need to give them a name. So let's make our three categories now.

Custom fields

Now that we have our categories, let's make some custom fields and associate them with our categories.

First, we need to decide what custom fields we need. Our gallery is to allow people to share information about their house partially to let them show off, and partially because it might be helpful to other people to hear about their experiences. This being said, we want to offer the users the opportunity to enter a fair bit of information. None of the information will be mandatory, so they can pick the fields they want to share.

We also have three types of fields we can choose from, a text field, a pull down field, and a list box field for multiple selections. We will also need to decide what kind of field each one is going to be.

Buildings

There are lots of things that could be both interesting and useful to know about a purchased building. Things such as:

- Age when acquired: pull down field — New, 0-5 years, 5-10 years, 10-20 Years, 20+ years
- Size: text field — this can be text to allow people to enter the real size in square meters, or just the number of rooms
- Location: text field — we don't want people to share their address, but a general location would be nice, for example Tokyo
- Cost: text field — this could be anything
- Agent: text field
- Agent Quality: pull down field — Excellent, Good, Average, Poor, Terrible
- Builder: text field
- Building Quality: pull down field — Excellent, Good, Average, Poor, Terrible
- Purchased: pull down field — Cash, Loan <50%, Loan >50%
- Bank Used: text field
- Quality: pull down field — Excellent, Good, Average, Poor, Terrible

That should give us a bit of information for our members.

Gardens

Gardens are less complex than buildings, but there is still some interesting information we can gather:

- Type: list box field—Garden, Water Feature, Path, Gate, Bonsai, Other
- Location: text field
- Construction: pull down field—DIY, Builder, Previous Owner
- Cost: text field
- Materials Purchased At: text field—for entering the name of the place they purchased from

Interior

Similar to gardens, interior features will also only have a few custom fields:

- Room Type: pull down field—Bedroom, Kitchen, Washitsu (Japanese Room), Lounge Room, Bathroom, Entrance, Hall, Other
- Construction: pull down field—DIY, Builder, Previous Owner
- Cost: text field
- Materials Purchased At: text field—for entering the name of the place they purchased from

Notice how some of our categories have identical fields, such as Location, Cost, Construction, and so on. Luckily, custom fields can be assigned to multiple categories so we can simply create the duplicate fields once and associate them to the required categories.

To create the custom fields, click the **Custom Fields** link in the menu at the top to bring up the **Custom Field Manager**. Now create a new custom field and fill in the required fields. The fields are all simple enough to fill in so we won't step through them.

Galleries

Now that we have our categories and our custom fields set up, it is time to put them to use in some galleries. Galleries are the containers for our actual gallery items (images and videos).

To create a new gallery, go to the **Gallery Manager** by clicking **Galleries** in the menu bar and then clicking **New**.

We will name our first gallery **Houses** and give it the category of **Buildings**. We don't need a description here right now. Hit **Save** and we will be given a screen to add a new entry to the gallery. We don't want to add one just yet, so just hit **Cancel** exit out.

We can now finish the rest of our galleries.

Settings

Now that we have laid out the structure of our Member Gallery, it's time to check the settings page. Click **Settings** in the menu to bring up the settings screen.

There are two tabs, **General** and **Frontend**. General only has one parameter which is the name of the overall gallery; we will put **Member Homes** in here.

Under the **Frontend** tab we have a few more options. Many of these are to help with either permissions or which features are enabled.

Let's set and confirm the following:

- **Frontend Upload**: Yes
- **Upload Group**: Select all of them except Public Frontend
- **Use Shadowbox**: Yes
- **Show Gallery Menu**: Show
- **Show Entry Count**: Show
- **Show Rating**: Show
- **Show Vote**: Show
- **Who Can Vote**: Registered — limit voting to registered
- **Show Comment Form**: Show
- **Who Can Comment**: Public
- **Show Comments**: Show

sh404SEF

Even though we are using sh404SEF, we won't be doing anything with it except the standard setup for which there are instructions included in the component itself. So, there is no need for us to add them here.

Under the default settings, sh404SEF will clean up our URLs and replace things like `cat=1` with `/renting/` and will also put a `.html` on the end of the last item in our URL to give the impression that it is an HTML page.

Other extensions

There are also a few smaller extensions that we still need to install and configure, but we should know enough by now to do them without guidance as long as we keep the purpose of our site in mind while doing so. Some we will cover later in other chapters.

- Ninja Shadowbox
- AllVideos
- MultiAds Plugin
- Ninjamonials
- JCE
- NinjaXplorer
- EasySQL
- JoomlaPack

Summary

This one was quite a long chapter with lots of heavy reading, but we should now have the most important extensions on our site configured and set up. We also have cleaned out the sample content and extensions that we don't need, and added sections and categories for our articles. We are ready now to start styling our site.

5
Installing and Modifying Templates

We now have the basics of our site in place, our extensions, but our site still looks quite bland. The default Joomla! appearance is nice enough, but not really what we want to represent our company. Also, there are probably thousands of sites with the same appearance. So we want to do something about the appearance and change it to something that will excite our visitors when they come to our site.

When we want to change the appearance of a Joomla! site, we will usually do it by installing a new template, and then modifying that template to meet our needs. So in this chapter we are going to have a look at how to:

- Find templates
- Choose templates
- Install new templates
- How to modify templates
- Why modifying templates is important

Finding a template

The easiest way to find Joomla! templates is in a "template club" or "template store".

A template club charges a fixed priced for access to their complete range of template downloads for a limited time, usually 3, 6, or 12 months. Note that some clubs also have a limit on the number of sites we can use the templates on as part of their license agreement.

Alternatively, there are also template stores that sell templates individually, but most Joomla! template sites use the club model. It would be very difficult to find, and list, all the Joomla! template clubs as new ones are starting all the time. Likewise, they occasionally close as well. However, we can list several of the more mainstream and popular clubs to give people an idea of what is available. Note that this list is in alphabetical order and is no reflection on the quality of the clubs mentioned.

- Joomla Bamboo (`http://www.joomlabamboo.com`)
- Joomla Junkies (`http://www.joomlajunkies.com`)
- Joomla Praise (`http://www.joomlapraise.com`)
- Joomla! Shack (`http://www.joomlashack.com`)
- Joomlart (`http://www.joomlart.com`)
- Ninja Theme (`http://ninjatheme.com`)
- Rocket Theme (`http://www.rockettheme.com`)

Choosing a template

When choosing a template, there are several factors we need to take into account. However, many people initially think about the wrong things, such as the colors and images present on the template. I consider these to be the wrong thing to focus on because:

- They are the simplest part of the template to change
- We should always modify the original colors and images at least a little bit unless we want our visitors to come to our site and think "Hey I know this template!," which will result in an immediate loss of respect for us and our business.

Instead we should not consider templates as finished product that we will install and leave as it is, but as a base upon which we will build and customize something unique to our site. So when evaluating a template we should be asking the following questions:

- Is it XHTML and CSS compliant?
- Does the overall shape and structure of the template match what I am looking for? For example, does it have the right number and placement of columns and module positions for what I want to achieve?
- What extra features does it have?

- Does it work in all major browsers?
- Does it have any extended typography?
- How does the template perform, speed wise?

XHTML and CSS validation

Most modern professional templates are valid XHTML and CSS, which means that they have been coded to fit to the standards set by the **World Wide Web Consortium (W3C)**. What this means to us is that the template is likely to continue to work in future browsers that support CSS and XHTML standards (most modern browsers). A web site that doesn't adhere to the standards may become distorted, or parts may even cease working correctly in future browsers.

Template structure

The template structure is far more important than the appearance because it can be quite difficult to change the structure of the template, especially for a non-expert, whereas the design and color scheme is usually much easier to change. When examining the structure, consider things like the column and module position placement.

When looking at a template we should always try to see the structure and imagine our own images and colors over it and think about if they match or not, rather than seeing the color and images and trying to restructure it.

Extra features

Most modern templates often include features like slideshows, tabs, sIFR (flash text replacement), pop-up images, fancy menus, and more. Often these extra features are powered by JavaScript, though some may be flash or even CSS.

If a template includes a lot of extra features, ensure that we want them, or at least that they can be disabled. This is because too many features can slow down a site, and they may conflict with the extensions we want to include in our site.

Browser compatibility

We should ensure that our template looks good in all popular browsers because our site visitors are very likely to use a variety of different browsers and we don't want to miss out on potential customers simply because they don't use the same web browser that we do.

The minimum browsers that a site should work with are:

- Firefox
- Internet Explorer 6, 7, and 8
- Safari
- Opera
- Google Chrome

These browsers form the overwhelming majority of traffic on the Internet and if we don't cater for at least them, we run the risk of losing customers.

Typography

Typography is an often underestimated part of template choice, and most modern templates include a wide array of typography including heading styles, alert boxes, quote styling, drop caps, formatted lists, and more. Having a wide array of Typography to choose from gives us much more flexibility in how we present our content without any extra work.

Template performance

Lots of extra features and a cool design are fine, but what if the template ends up taking 3 minutes to load on a broadband connection? When considering a template, we should consider who our intended audience is and what their average Internet connection is going to be, and evaluate the "weight" of a template accordingly. The weight refers to the total download size required for it to display, this includes images, JavaScript, CSS, and other media files.

Generally, the more features and the fancier the design, the heavier a template is, though this may not always be the case.

Installing a template

Templates can be installed like any other extension, simply click **Extensions | Install/Uninstall** and then select the template ZIP file on our computer and install it.

To set a template as our primary template, go to the template manager, **Extensions | Template Manager**, select the checkbox for our template, and click the **Default** button in the top-right-hand corner.

Alternatively, if we want different templates on different pages, we can use the **Menu Assignment** option in the **Template Manager**.

Modifying a template

Before we look at modifying a template, we need to choose a template for our sample site.

There are many free and commercial templates out there, and originally I intended to choose a template that we could distribute with the book, but after looking at some of the clubs I mentioned above, and knowing that our site is going to be a real site, I found the Vertigo template at Rocket Theme, and it fits really well with our sample site plans. Our site is aimed at helping people with housing and real estate, so something that feels light and open, like a well-designed house, will probably feel better for our customers, putting them in a good mood while browsing the site. The cloudy style with the light blue, white, and green definitely captures this feeling well.

However, as mentioned above, we want to make at the very least some image changes to our template so that it is more personal and isn't immediately recognizable as a template. Unfortunately, the parallax effect at the top of the page is pretty unique and so it will be difficult to make the template completely unique, but we can certainly make a few changes to personalize it. Let's start with replacing some images.

Template images

Editing and replacing images is the easiest way to make some changes to the appearance of our web site, and almost anyone can do it with the right software. Many modern web sites use a lot of images as important parts of their design, and this has both advantages and disadvantages.

The primary advantage is that our site will potentially look a lot nicer than one done with just CSS colors, as we can do things like rounded corners, gradients, and shadows on our images.

There are however several considerations that we must keep in mind when working with images, so that they are used correctly and without a negative impact on our site.

Image considerations

Some of the main considerations when working with images are:

- Compression and format
- When images aren't visible
- Originality and copyright

Image compression and formats

Regardless of anything we do, images will slow down the site because a user has to download the images they need when they visit a page. This can make the loading of a page much slower than the same page without any images. This is less of a concern if most of our users are on broadband Internet connections and have modern browsers that will cache downloaded images instead of downloading them for every page.

We can also reduce the impact of this by choosing the right sizes, resolutions, and formats for our images.

There are three main image formats that we will see used on the Web, JPG (or JPEG), GIF, and PNG. Each of these serves a different purpose.

JPG files can show a lot of detail and have the smallest file size, but they are less sharp in the detail they hold, and every time we edit and save a JPG, it loses a little bit of detail as it is compressed. They are best used for larger images or where sharpness and definition are less important, such as photographs or background images.

GIF is an older format and not as widely used as it once was. It also produces larger files than JPG. Its main advantages are that it produces sharper images, partially supports transparency, and also supports animation.

PNG is a format designed to replace GIF, and has many similarities to it. One of the important differences between the two is that PNG files come in a number of bit depths: 8bit, 24bit, and 32bit. The higher bit depth PNGs have improved color, sharpness, and transparency support, but also larger file sizes. 32bit PNGs, for example, support partial transparency, where an image can be seen through to the one below it, like colored glass, whereas 8bit PNGs (and GIFs) only support 100% or 0% transparency, so it can only be clear glass, or no glass.

A modern web site will usually have a combination of PNG and JPG files, with GIF files used sparingly. The PNG files will also often vary between 8-24-32bit depending on the level of detail in the image, and if transparency is needed or not.

It is very important to note that the partial transparency of 32bit PNG files is not supported by default in Internet Explorer 6, and transparent areas show up as a dirty blue grey. There are a number of JavaScript and CSS hacks to fix this however, and most modern templates include one by default. However, GIF and 8bit PNG transparency works as expected.

When producing images for our site, we should try to save them in exactly the dimensions we want them to be. Even though we can change the size of an image via CSS, doing so can have negative consequences. For example, shrinking an image via CSS will mean the image is larger than it needs to be and thus, the page takes longer to load. Enlarging it via CSS will remove sharpness from the image as it expands.

Also, pay attention to the resolution of the image. For example, images taken with a digital camera, even though they might be the right dimensions for our site, will usually have a very high resolution. The files will now be larger and slower than they need to be. Often a digital photo can be reduced to 20-50% of its original resolution without making a noticeable difference to its appearance. The result being much smaller image files.

When images aren't visible

Images may not be visible to people with vision impairments, those who use screen readers, or people who have images turned off in their browsers. As a result, images should be used carefully when they are included in critical features, like site navigation, so as to not block out certain sections of the community if they can't see them.

This can be alleviated through the careful application of `alt` and `title` attributes to `<img>` tags so that visitors with vision impairments or images disabled can make sense of our site.

> The `alt` and `title` attributes can only be added to image elements, which have an `<img>` tag, but not to background images that are specified on `div`s or other HTML tags. `title` attributes can - actually be added to some other elements, such as links, but the `title` refers to the element in this case, and not the background image.

To add `alt` and `title` attributes to an image, we will need to edit the PHP file which displays the image, usually `index.php` for templates, and find the `<img>` tag, which will look something like `<img src="/media/images/mylogo.png" />` then add the attributes to the tag to make it look more like:

```
<img src="/media/images/mylogo.png" alt="A logo image of a Japanese
style house and the words Your Japanese House" title="Your Japanese
House" />.
```

From this we can see that the `alt` attribute should contain a relevant description of the appearance of the image, whereas the title contains something to deliver the meaning of the image, in this case our site logo. `title`s can be seen when a visitor moves their cursor over the image. `alt` text will only be seen by a screen reader, if images are disabled, or on mouse over in replacement to the `title` attribute if one hasn't been specified.

Originality and copyright

An issue that often pops up for novice and DIY web developers is that of image copyright. When looking for images for our site, it is very easy to hop onto a search service like Google Images and look around for some images we like, then download and use these images for our own site, or even worse to link directly to an image hosted on someone else's site.

Warning:

Copying copyrighted images from other sites is more common than most people realize, but it is still legally considered a form of theft. Doing so can potentially result in a lawsuit for us. Even if it doesn't get that far, then at the very least a quick email to our hosting company will be likely to get our site taken down and our account suspended.

If we are not artistically inclined enough to make all our own images, then there are still a number of web sites dedicated to selling stock images to be used in web sites, such as http://www.istockphoto.com. While it will cost a few dollars per image, at least we can rest safely, knowing that we won't get a nasty letter from a lawyer or have our site vanish over night.

It should also be mentioned that we should attempt to keep some consistency in the style of images used on our site. If the styles deviate too far from each other, then it will become obvious that they are stock images and look amateurish, which will cost us credibility.

This is especially important with illustrations and cartoons, as the style is much more obvious. Photos are more difficult to distinguish, but care should still be taken.

Finding and modifying images

When working with templates, it is usually a good idea to work with two copies. A local copy kept on our work computer, where changes can be made quickly and easily, and the live copy that is installed on our site. This way we can make changes locally and upload them to the site.

Once we have our two copies ready, we need to find the images that we want to edit. They will usually be in an images directory, but there may be several sub directories into which they are divided. This is especially true for templates that come with several styles by default.

Also, many images may appear very similar in the file system thumbnails, making it difficult to work out which image is from which part of the template without opening them all up.

Thankfully, however, we have Firefox and Firebug, which we mentioned in earlier chapters. We can just right-click on an img element or another element type that has a background image, and select **Inspect Element** to get the information we need.

For an img element we look in the left hand pane to see the img tag itself and the src attribute, which contains our image location. For background images, we can look in the right-hand pane and find the CSS entries for background or background-image. These will tell us exactly where to look.

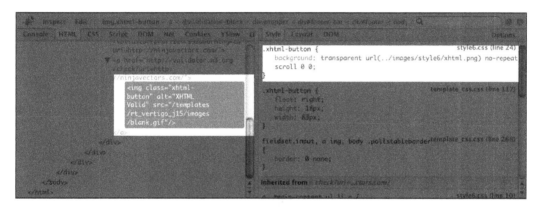

Once we have found our images we can replace them or edit them using an image editor. As mentioned before, the recommended image editor is Adobe Fireworks. It has a very intuitive interface, can handle most popular image formats, can do vector or bitmap editing, and can output different quality PNG files: 8, 24, and 32 bit.

Vector and bitmap images

When working with images we should become familiar with two terms, **bitmap** and **vector**. Bitmap images are images that are drawn literally using a map of colored dots. Each point on the image has a color assigned to it. Vector images, however, have the image composed of separate objects that have corner points and information regarding how to color and fill the space between the corner points.

Vector images have the benefit of being much easier to scale up and down, as the points are just scaled and then filled in, so they retain all their original detail no matter how large or small they are made, and can be resized indefinitely.

Bitmap images, however, need to expand or shrink the color map they use. So if a bitmap is shrunk, it loses its detail as different points are merged together. If enlarged, they become fuzzy and blurry as what was once a single point of color now covers multiple points with the same color. The consolation for this though is that bitmap files usually have much smaller file sizes than vector images, and most web browsers can't display vector image file types at all.

Generally, vector art is used for original and master illustrations, and from the vector images, bitmap images are produced in the desired sizes for actual use.

JPG, GIF, and PNG are all usually bitmap images. The one exception to these is Adobe Fireworks native PNG files. Native Fireworks PNG files can store layer information and vector information, allowing them to be edited many times. When viewed on a web site, however, they look and act like a normal PNG file. However, they have extremely large file size compared to a **flattened** bitmap PNG file. So we should never use a Fireworks PNG file on our web site, but instead flatten them into a different PNG bitmap image (using the **Save As** option in Fireworks).

Modifying our sample site images

For our sample site, the main images we need to replace are the clouds in the showcase area. We might also want to change the grass at the bottom of the page but it should be fine as it is, the showcase is the important one.

An advantage with this template is that apart from the showcase and grass, the rest of it is mainly white; thereby reducing the number of images we need to change.

Logos

The first thing we want to change is the site logo, as it is from the style of the logo, which is effectively our brand that we will draw much of our site art.

Our logo should be well thought out and professionally designed, if we want to be successful. Few things can make us seem more untrustworthy and unprofessional than a bad logo. Changing our logo after a few months is also not usually a good idea as we need to rebuild our customer confidence once again. In the marketing world, the power of a brand is well understood, and many companies spend far more on marketing to improve their brand perception than they do on research and development to improve their products. So, we should put a significant amount of effort into the design of our logo.

Logos should look good at any size, as we may want to put it in icons or at the bottom of our page, or even on t-shirts and hats. As a result, photos are almost always a bad idea for a logo as they don't scale well. Photos also *age* more quickly than an illustrated logo. Will that shirt we are wearing still look fashionable in a year's time? What about five?

Photos also make it difficult to transfer a logo into other mediums, such as making hats, t-shirts, or business cards where every different color equals an increase in difficulty and cost. So photos are out.

We might be able to make our logo ourselves if we have some choose to use artistic skills, or leave it to a professional. It is possible to get professional logos for as little as $99 from web sites like `http://www.logodesignguru.com`. So it is strongly suggested using one of these services over making our own unless we are very confident in our skills.

Luckily, we have an in-house artist that will be helping us with our logo, and also with some of our other graphics.

As our site is going to be called *Your Japanese House* and is about housing in Japan, it naturally follows that our logo should be something related to Japanese Housing.

After a chat with our artist, we have selected a traditional Japanese style house image that we will shrink down for the logo, but also use on our site showcase in a larger form.

Then to go with the image we need some text. *Your Japanese House* is quite long, so a horizontal logo will take up a lot of useful space. Instead, we will try the text vertically on three lines with one word per line.

With all the text the same size, we still end up with either tiny text or a huge logo. Instead, let's focus on one main word "Japanese" and keep it larger, while shrinking the others to make them fit.

Now let's look at our image with the resized text.

Next, we will put a slight tint on the lettering to give it a slightly less flat appearance, and find a nice oriental feeling font. Now, we have a spiffy logo.

One concern I have is that the house won't scale down much smaller than it is without losing too much detail, so perhaps it was too detailed an image for the logo. However, I am not likely to need it any smaller as I don't foresee us producing key rings or caps for the site, so we should be ok.

Once our logo is complete, we can upload it to the server using our FTP client.

When working with the images for our template, we will always need to reload the page to see the new images. Sometimes, however, even reloading doesn't work, and the old image will still be displayed. This is because of the browser caching the images that it downloads and then loading them later from the hard drive of our computer and not downloading them to the site, to give performance improvements. In this case, we will need to clear our browser cache then reload the page again.

To clear our cache in Firefox, select **Tools | Clear Private Data**, uncheck everything except **Cache** and then press **Clear Private Data Now**.

For other browsers, it will usually be under the **Tools** or **Options** menu.

The showcase area images

As mentioned above, we want to use the cloud style but we will replace the clouds in the showcase with something more relevant to our site. The overall parallax effect is nifty, so we will leave it and work with similar images.

The first thing we need to do is find all the images that we need to edit, and then decide what to do with them.

Looking at the template we can see that there are at least four images overlaid on top of each other: the very front, static image, and the three layers behind it, of the moving images.

Using Firebug again, we can just right-click on the showcase and use **Inspect Element** to find out where these images are. Looking at the HTML structure in the left pane, we can see five `div` tags nested inside each other with the following `id` attributes:

- showcase-layer1
- showcase-layer2
- showcase-layer3
- showcase-bottom-bg
- showcase-bottom

If we click on each of these, we will find that there are in fact five images which we need to edit and not just four, with the fifth one being the white gradient border at the base of the showcase. Looking at the CSS in the right-hand pane, we can see that all our images are in either the /images/theme1 folder or the /images/style1 folder.

Using Fireworks we will open these images, replace their contents with our new images, save them, and then use our FTP program to upload them to the web server.

Our artist has produced for us another two houses, some clouds, a hill, and some different garden plants for us to use in our images. Therefore, we will put the clouds in the back ground, and the plants and houses on the hill in the main image.

Because our artist did all the images as vectors, we can resize them easily without losing any detail, allowing us to change them to suit the size of the showcase.

After assembling our new images, new clouds, and a green main area with the hill, houses and plants on it, we can again upload them via FTP to our server.

If we wanted to continue changing images for our site, such as the footer grass, or the icons for the module class suffixes, we would simply follow the same procedures outlined above.

Favicon

One image we can't forget is our **favicon**. A favicon (short for favorites icon) is the small 16x16 pixel icon that is displayed to the left of the URL bar at the top of the browser. The default favicon for a Joomla! site is the Joomla! logo and can be found in the base Joomla! directory as the file favicon.ico. The best way I have found for generating a favicon is to make a 16x16 or 32x32 PNG file and then use an online favicon generator such as the one at http://tools.dynamicdrive.com/favicon/ to upload and convert the image into the correct format and size.

We can then download the image from the site, and upload it to our web site. We should then be able to clear our cache and see the new favicon. At least now our web site won't be too easy to spot as that of a Joomla! web site.

 Favicons are persistent little images, and sometimes even clearing the cache will not get the new favicon to appear with some browsers. If we are sure that we uploaded the favicon, but can't get it to appear, we should try a different browser or computer that hasn't accessed the site before. It should update correctly within a couple of hours or days.

Template PHP

Generally, the PHP we encounter in a template will be simpler than that in extensions. This is because the purpose of a template is usually just to put a particular style onto our site and not to perform actions other than loading our extensions on each page.

Recently, however, Joomla! templates have expanded in complexity, particularly in the area of menus and sometimes in extra features usually left to extensions such as module or image sliders. So the need to know PHP in order to edit our template has increased.

Editing PHP files

When we want to edit our PHP, we can do it in one of two places, on our local computer and then upload it, or do it remotely on the server itself via any number of editing tools, or via the **Template Manager** screen.

If done via the **Template Manager** screen, we will only be able to modify the `index.php` and we also won't have a local copy of the changes on our computer. So if we upload a new copy of the `index.php` file, then we will potentially overwrite and remove our changes with a new file.

As a result, the best method is usually to make the changes on our local computer and upload the files as we did with the images.

Editing our sample site's PHP

Even though it is not often that we will want to change the PHP of a template, there is one thing we do want to change in our case.

The parallax effect in the showcase is a nice effect, but after we have seen it once, it will serve only to be a distraction to most people as they navigate deeper into the site. As a result, we want to enable it only on the front page, by disabling it on all other pages.

How do we do this? Well first, we will need to check the current page URL, and if it is anything except the home page, `http://yourjapanesehouse.com`, then we would disable the effect.

Thanks to the Joomla! API, there are a lot of Joomla! functions we can call to automatically perform common tasks, such as retrieving the current URL that can be done with a simple call to the `JURI::current()` function. This function will return the current URL complete with `http://` (or `https://`), and if we need it, a trailing slash.

Luckily, our template has a parameter that we can change to enable (two different enable states) or disable the effect. If we can intercept this parameter before the template uses it, we can change it to any value we like.

The parameter is loaded at the top of the template with the following line of code:

```
$enable_parallax=$this->params->get("enableParallax","full page");
```

Looking at the function call, we can see full page as the default for the parameter which implies to us that the real value for each of the parameters is a lowercase copy of the display value used in the template parameter form. In this case, the display value from the parameter form is Full Page. So we want to use disabled as the parameter value to turn off our parallax effect.

So now we will wrap the parameter loading code in the if statement, and disable it if our URL is not our home page. The final code will look like this:

```
if (JURI::current() == 'http://yourjapanesehouse.com/' ){

  $enable_parallax = $this->params->get("enableParallax", "full
    page");

} else {

  $enable_parallax = 'disabled';

}
```

Now we can upload our index.php file and our parallax effect will only activate on the home page. Our visitors can have a bit of a fun playing on the home page, but won't be distracted deeper into the site.

For now that is all we need to do with our template PHP. Next is CSS.

Template CSS

The next thing we will look at is editing our template CSS to make our site a little nicer looking. Templates will always have at least one CSS file, template_css. css, but may have others. Commonly, modern templates will also have a CSS file specifically for IE 6, another for IE 7 (as they almost always require some special tweaking) and then one for each style variation, if there is more than one style for the template.

Editing CSS files

Just like our PHP files we can edit our CSS file in one of two places, on our local computer and then upload it, or do it remotely on the server. A slight difference here though is that if the **Template Manager** screen is used, editing the CSS will give us a choice of which file, if more than one, to edit.

Also like our PHP, the best method is to edit it on our local computer and then upload the files. This way we have a master copy in a safe place.

Editing our sample site's CSS

Before we dive into editing our CSS, we need to decide exactly what we want to change. Looking over the site and viewing a couple of different pages, will want to make four initial obvious changes. They are:

1. Move the logo up slightly, so that it no longer runs over the top of the tree.
2. Change all links to the same green color, as currently some are blue.
3. Change the color of the bullets from blue to something that matches better.
4. Stop the lines in the menu module on the left from touching the main area.

It is easiest to see them on the weblinks page, as shown:

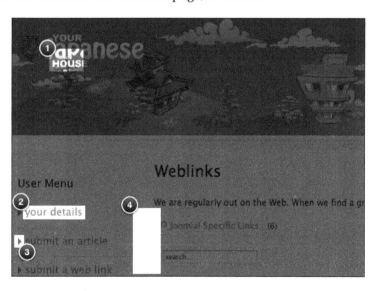

To start making changes, we will once again use Firebug and Inspect Element. This way we not only find out which files and lines we need to edit, but we can also test our changes live on the screen to see what they will look like before we write them into the files.

Let's start with the logo.

Right-click and select **Inspect Element**. Looking in the right pane, we can see, amongst the other CSS affecting this element:

```
#logo {                                    template_css.css (line 4)
height:72px;
left:0;
position:absolute;
top:20px;
width:225px;
}
```

Looking at this, and keeping in mind that we want to move the logo up slightly, we can see that the `top` CSS rule is the one that we most likely want to change. The rule `top` indicates how many pixels down from the top of the enclosing HTML element, our logo is.

If we now left-click the area where `20px` is written, we will find that we can now edit this value. We will change it to `10px` and see what happens. Like magic, the logo moves up 10 pixels. This looks better, but is still not enough. If we try `0px` next, then we will find that it is in an almost perfect position.

It is pointless to have `top:0px;` in our CSS, unless we need to change it from another value to 0. So let's see how we go without the rule altogether. Right-click anywhere over `top:0px;` and select **Delete "top"**. The `top` CSS rule should vanish altogether, and because there are no other rules to replace it, our logo will just sit where it is, at the default `top` value of `0` which is where we want it.

Now we need to make the change permanent. Since Firebug only allows us to edit the copy of the page which we have downloaded, it doesn't affect the copy on the server.

If we look back in our right-hand Firebug pane, at the top-right of our CSS, we will see `template_css.css (line 4)`. This tells us the file and line that our CSS can be found on, in this case in the `template_css.css` file on line 4. How convenient is that!

So now we can edit our file, delete this CSS rule completely, then upload it, and if we refresh our page, viola our logo is in the right position.

Now if we Inspect Element our blue links, we will see the following:

```
ul.menu a, ul.menu .separator {          style1.css (line 58)
color:#21607F;
}
```

If we move our mouse over the CSS rule, we will see a small gray circle with a line through it that we may have noticed when previously editing our logo. This symbol is usually used to indicate "no" for something, and in this case it indicates that we can disable a CSS rule without deleting it entirely like we did with `top:0px`. Click the grey "no" symbol and we will see that it turns red, and our links have turned green. This is because there is some other CSS for our links that turns them green, before this particular style is applied which turns them blue. By disabling the CSS rule in this way we can see how our page would look if it didn't exist.

Now that we know that we want to remove this CSS rule as well, we can find the file and line, make the change, and upload the file.

Now for our bullets! These bullets are actually images, so they won't have changed with our text. Now we could make our own bullets for the site, but unless there is an absolute need to, we don't want to spend time on it.

If we **Inspect Element** on the bullets, we can't see any information about a background image. In fact, it seems to be pretty bare. If we look to the left Firebug pane, we can see that an `li` element (abbreviation for list item), is selected and there is a small arrow next to it. The arrow indicates there are elements inside this element, and if we click on it they will open up.

Inside our `li` is an `a` tag (the "a" is an abbreviation for anchor, and is usually used as a weblink or bookmark) and then inside that is a `span` tag. If we click on the `a` tag (right on the `a` itself), we can now see our background image information.

```
ul.menu a, ul.menu .separator {          style1.css (line 58)
background:transparent url(../images/style1/submenu-arrow.png) no-
repeat scroll 0 16px;
}
```

Looking at this, we can see the image location and could now edit it if we wish. But knowing that our template has various styles, we may as well test to see if any of them have bullets that match our site.

Click directly on the URL (. . ./images...) in the right pane. Now we will change the /style1/ to /style2/. Our bullets have just their changed color to brown. Conveniently, this matches our style, and if we check the rest of the styles we will find that brown is the one that matches best. So even though we are using `style 1` in our template, we can happily pull images from other styles if we wish, just by changing our CSS.

Let's put the changes into the right file and upload them.

Lastly, we want to put some more space between the menu item underlines in the left column and the main body.

If we do **Inspect Element** on our menu items again, we can see that they have an interesting `margin` rule.

```
ul.menu li {                        template_css.css (line 223)
border-bottom:1px solid #E6E6E6;
float:none;
list-style-image:none;
list-style-position:outside;
list-style-type:none;
margin:0 -15px;
padding:0 15px;
}
```

The `margin` of `0 -15px` will give them a `0` pixel margin (basically no margin) on the top and bottom, and `-15` pixels on both sides. This is most likely our culprit.

Margins, padding, and several other CSS rules respond to all four directions and can have values entered for each direction individually, starting from top and moving clockwise : top, right, bottom, left. Alternatively, they can have their values abbreviated if they repeat. For example, 10px 10px 10px 10px can be abbreviated to simply 10px. If an abbreviation of two values is entered, then the first value is used for both the top and bottom, and the other for left and right, just like our `margin` in this case.

If we want to remove the negative `15` pixel margin from the right but not from the left, we will have to remove the abbreviation and replace it with two different values. Let's change the margin to:

```
margin:0 0 0 -15px;
```

Sure enough, our lines have moved back from the center of our template and look a lot better. The end result of this CSS work is below, a much better looking site.

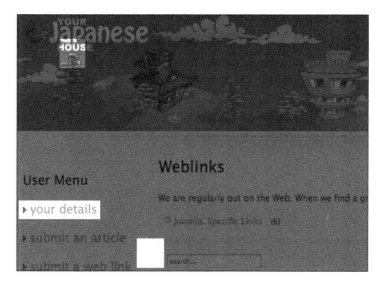

Summary

With that, we have finished the template for our sample site, and our introduction to templates. We should now be able to find, modify, and customize our templates. Editing the images, PHP, and CSS to give us the type of site that we want.

We also found out that it's important for us to edit our template and not just leave it as the default, so that we don't risk losing the respect of our visitors.

Next we will look at Modules and how to make them work for our site.

6
Customizing Modules

The next thing we will look at are modules, an important and useful part of our site development. We are going to look at how modules operate, and how to configure and customize them to meet our needs.

Specifically, we want to add some modules to our sample site, and then make changes to them so that they better meet our needs.

First, we will look at how modules are constructed and how they operate, then we will look at the customization process, which will consist of:

- Understanding the existing code
- Planning our changes
- Implementing our changes

As we go through these activities, we will practice by customizing a module for our site.

Module construction and operation

Unlike components, which typically are different on every page they appear, modules are small, independent programs that usually appear with the same output on multiple pages of our site.

Modules rarely perform major functions, and usually provide summaries, links to other information, or extra minor features to our site. Modules are executed separately to components, so they cannot pass information directly between each other. As a result, modules are always self-contained, though they may reference tables or files used by components or even other modules. They are also usually displayed on the edges of our site, with the main component or content in the center.

The most simple a module can be is two files. One is an XML file (also called a **manifest file**), which contains information about the module, such as file lists and parameters that tell Joomla! how to handle the module. The other is a PHP file, and it is in the PHP file that all the code for the execution of the module is inserted.

From here, modules get more and more complex. They can include other PHP files, images, JavaScript, or CSS files as needed to get the result we want.

To get output from the module to appear on our site, it will need to be programmed either as text strings in `echo` or `print` commands or inline HTML, where the HTML is written outside the PHP opening and closing tags `<?php` and `?>`. For example, look at the following code snippet:

```php
<?php

$myName = "Daniel";
$myJob = "Web Developer";

echo '<div>My name is '.$myName.'</div><br />';

?>
<div>My job is <?php echo $myJob; ?></div>
```

Module in a module

As Joomla! development practices have advanced, the demands placed on all aspects of Joomla! development have increased, including those placed upon modules. Developers began to desire more control over when and how modules were displayed without hacking the Joomla! core or their templates. For example, by only showing certain modules to certain user groups, browsers, or even to certain individual users.

However, templates always show the modules that the Joomla! core passes to them and can't control individual modules, only module positions. Also, the Joomla! core has only limited options for displaying modules, such as restricting a module to a certain access group or above (but not the reverse) and restricting it to certain menu item pages.

Sometimes, templates can be modified to perform extra filtering of modules. However, any changes are restricted to specific module positions, and moving them or changing the requirements requires recoding the template again.

As a result of these roadblocks, the practice of loading one or more modules inside another module came into being.

The thought behind this was that the outer module would always be displayed, but would be styled so as to be invisible. Then the outer module manually loads the inner modules one by one and applies the special conditions, formatting, or tests that are required.

This allowed modules to be filtered by special requirements, or have special styling applied, without the need to modify the template or Joomla! core.

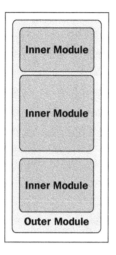

Styling the outer module to be hidden is usually done via giving the outer module a Module Class suffix of something like **-hidden** or something else that has no reference in the site's CSS stylesheet. This will remove most, if not all of the styling, from the outer module. If combined with turning off the display of the outer module's title, the module will be effectively invisible.

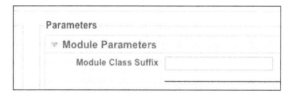

Module customization

When we start out as a Joomla! developer, it is often much easier, and takes a lot less time, to edit an existing extension that does most of what we want than it is to create a completely new one. So, we will find some extensions that almost fit what we want to do, and then modify them to fill the gaps.

Modifying top ten members

Even though this is outside of our goals list, we want to put up some simple modules to fill up the site with interesting information. Since, we want to encourage people to participate in the forum, it might be worth putting in some modules that show our top posters and rewarding them with having their name up on the site.

Looking around on the JED, we can find a recent threads module, but there is no top posters module for Joo!BB. There is, however, one for Fireboard, another popular Joomla! Forum component, called **Fireboard Top 10 Active 10**. So we will take that one, and modify it to use Joo!BB, and just show the top 10 posters instead.

Step 1: Understanding the existing code

If we open up the ZIP file `mod_fbmodule.zip`, we will find a number of files contained within it. Let's look at each file and its purpose.

Luckily, this module has been created using the recommended partially MVC style, so it will make a good model to study.

en-GB.mod_fbmodule.ini

This file is what is called a language file, and is used to make an extension easily translatable, and also to make any visible text easily editable.

By gathering all the visible text from an extension in one place, it is a lot more convenient than having to search through many files to find the text you want to change or translate.

Language files are named according to a strict naming standard, as this allows Joomla! to access the appropriate files quickly and easily.

The naming being:

```
<language>-<locale>.<extension_name>.ini
```

With `<language>` being a lower case, two-letter abbreviation, `<locale>` being an upper case two-letter abbreviation, and `<extension>` being the system name for the extension.

So in our file above we have the name `en-GB.mod_fbmodule.ini`, which indicates that the language is **English**, the locale is **Great Britain**, and it is for the extension **mod_fbmodule**.

Before we move into our actual program code, let's check the file and make any changes that we need in order for our module text to display accurately.

If we open the file, we see the following:

```
TYPE OF USER=User Type
DESC OF USER=If 'Top' displays the top posters, If 'Active' displays
the active poster
TOP POSTER=%s
NO OF USERS=No of users
DESC NO OF USERS=Number of user entries to display
NO OF POSTS=%s
FB ITEM ID=FB Item Id
DESC FB ITEM ID=Fire bord Item id (menu ite id)
```

The capitalized text to the left-hand side is the **Key** and the text to the right is the **Value** associate with that Key. Whenever the Joomla! translation code comes across the Key in some text it is translating, then it replaces that Key with the Value listed in this file.

Whenever we are editing an existing extension, we will probably want to avoid changing the Keys because if we do, then we need to search through all our files to find them. Luckily, our users won't see the keys anyway so even if they have strange names it is not a problem.

Looking at the Values, we can see four changes that we will want to make. First, we will change the two Fireboard references into Joo!BB. Then, we need to fix the two spelling mistakes in the last line.

We can also remove the TYPE OF USER and DESC OF USER Keys, because we don't need the active poster option, we just want the top posters.

Our final language file should look like this:

```
TOP POSTER=%s
NO OF USERS=No of users
DESC NO OF USERS=Number of user entries to display
NO OF POSTS=%s
FB ITEM ID=Joo!BB Item Id
DESC FB ITEM ID=Joo!BB Item id (menu item id)
```

helper.php

As the name indicates, this file contains code which can be used to help our module do its job. It's often a good idea to split auxiliary actions, such as database calls and calculations out of our main module file to make them cleaner and easier to understand, and bundle those into a helper file.

Looking over the code, there are three main sections all inside the class `ModFbModule`. There are two functions at the top, `getTopPosters` and `getActivePosters`. Below that, a large chunk of commented code, with a function in its `getItems`.

This large commented section is of no use to us, as it is just old code, so let's delete it to clean up the helper file. Make sure not to delete the closing parenthesis, },
at the bottom.

Also noticeable is the lack of PHP closing tag in the file. To fix this, create a new line at the bottom of the file, and add `?>` to that line.

The two functions are used to generate our lists of users depending on if we want the top or most active posters. We don't need the `getActivePosters` function anymore, so we will remove it shortly.

index.html

This is a blank file and is here for security reasons to stop people directly viewing this directory on the server. Another one appears in the `tmpl` folder for the same reason.

mod_fbmodule.php

This is the primary file for our module and it is from here that all our other files will be called.

Opening up the file which is relatively short, let's step through each of the major commands and see what they do.

```
defined('_JEXEC') or die('Direct Access not allowed.');
```

This line is for security and should appear at the top of every PHP file on your site. This is to prevent people from calling the files directly without going through the Joomla! framework first. You **must** make sure you put this line at the top of any PHP files you write. Otherwise, you risk your site being hacked.

```
require_once(dirname(__FILE__).DS.'helper.php');
```

This line loads our helper file that we just looked at. We need to load it so that we can call the functions contained within it. The `dirname(__FILE__)` function returns the directory that the current executing file resides in.

```
$usertype = $params->get('user_type');
$noofusers = $params->get('no_of_users');
$fbitemid = $params->get('fb_item_id');
```

These three lines access some of the parameters for this extension, and get the values so we can use them as follows:

```
if ($usertype==0) {
  $items = ModFbModule::getTopPosters($noofusers,$fbitemid);
}else{
  $items = ModFbModule::getActivePosters($noofusers,$fbitemid);
}
```

Here is the crucial part of our code. We check the `$usertype` parameter and depending on the value, we either get our top posters or active posters by calling the helper functions, and passing them the remaining parameters.

We will need to alter this later so that it no longer loads the `$usertype` variable or calls the `getActivePosters` function.

The results of the function, an array of objects, is then placed into the `$items` variable.

```
require(JModuleHelper::getLayoutPath('mod_fbmodule'));
```

`JModuleHelper` is a Joomla! class that contains several functions which we can use to speed up module development. `getLayoutPath` is one of those functions and will use the variables present in the Joomla! framework to find and return the path to the layout file for the module (which we will look at next).

Once the layout file is loaded, it will take the data inside the `$items` variable and lay it out how we want it displayed.

/tmpl/default.php

This is our module layout file. The layout code has been separated from the logic code to make it easier to modify one without affecting the other. For example, we can create multiple layout files and then only call the one that we want on a particular page. This is something that wouldn't have been possible if the logic and layout were merged together.

So now let's look at the code in the file.

```
<?php defined('_JEXEC') or die('Restricted access'); // no direct
access ?>
```

This is our expected security line, to stop people executing this file outside of Joomla!.

```
<table width="100%" cellpadding="2" cellspacing="2" border=0>
<tr>
<td style="text-align:left" width="70%"><b>Member</b></td>
<td style="text-align:right" width="30%"><b>Posts</b></td>
</tr>
```

These lines start an HTML table that is then used to layout the member and posts information. It also creates one row, with the `tr` tag, and two data cells, `td` tags, in that row. The two cells show the headings for our `Member` and `Posts` columns.

```
<tr><td height="4"></td></tr>
```

This next line is just an empty cell and appears to simply be a spacer parameter between the headings and the data.

```
<?php foreach ($items as $item) { ?>
<tr>
<td style="text-align:left">

<a   href='index.php?option=com_fireboard&func=fbprofile&task=showprf&I
temid=<?php echo $item->fbitemid; ?>&userid=<?php echo $item->userid;
?>'><?php echo JText::sprintf('TOP POSTER', $item->name); ?></a>

</td>

<td style="text-align:right">
<?php echo JText::sprintf('NO OF POSTS', $item->total); ?>
</td>
</tr>
<?php } ?>
```

Now we are into the most important part of our layout file. This is the section where our data is output. First, we start a `foreach` loop that will go through our `$items` variable, which was filled up with data in our `mod_fbmodule.php` file, and then outputs an HTML table row and two cells with our data inside them.

In the data cells, we have some function calls: `JText::sprintf('TOP POSTER', $item->name);` and `JText::sprintf('NO OF POSTS', $item->total);`. The `JText` class contains lots of useful functions for accessing the information in our language file, which we looked at earlier. In this case we are using the `sprintf` function, which is used to get the language Value matching the Key in the first parameter. It then replaces any special markers in that text with the values passed in the second and subsequent parameters.

So what does that actually mean? Let's look at a specific example to clear this up. First, let's go back to our language file, `en-GB.mod_fbmodule.ini`, and look for the Value matching our first Key, `TOP POSTER`. Looking in our language file, we find the following:

```
TOP POSTER=%s
```

So the Value for TOP POSTER is %s. The %s is our special marker that will be replaced by the JText::sprintf function. It is replaced with the second value passed into the function, which is $item->name, containing the name of one of our users.

This sort of technique is useful if you want to embed your results into some text without having to cut the text up into multiple pieces. But for us, we just want the raw data in a list so this is overkill for us this time.

Inside the data cells is also a web link defined by the a element. Currently this link points to fireboard, so we will need to change it later as well.

```
</table>
```

The last line closes off our table and finishes our file.

Before we move to the next file though, something that needs to be pointed out is that currently, a lot of formatting CSS has been hard-coded into our layout file. This is mainly for the text alignment and widths of our table cells. Look at the following example:

```
<td style="text-align:left">
<td style="text-align:left" width="70%">
```

CSS should always be in separate files, if possible, or written into the <head> section of our page (controlled by the templates on Joomla! sites) and not written inline into our HTML tags. This is because inline CSS is much harder to find than if it was in a CSS file. It also means that the same CSS information needs to be written out multiple times, once for every time it is used, instead of just once in the CSS file. Having to write it out every time makes it difficult to make adjustments to large sections of the page.

Also, b tags have been used around the title text for our table to make them bold. b tags have been replaced by strong tags as this is more semantically correct. So b tags shouldn't be used either as they may potentially be removed from HTML definitions in the future. To keep our web site future proof, we will later replace these with strong tags. Or even better, replace the existing td elements and the b elements both with just th elements, which indicate a table header, instead of bolded td (table cell) elements like they are now.

mod_fbmodule.xml

This XML file is the **Extension Manifest**. It contains all the information Joomla! needs to install and manage the extension and it's files. This file is reasonably long, but many of the XML elements are self-explanatory, so we will only focus on the sections that are important to us.

```
<files>

<!-- The "module" attribute signifies that this is the main controller
file -->
<filename module="mod_fbmodule">mod_fbmodule.php</filename>
                <filename>index.html</filename>
                <filename>helper.php</filename>
                <filename>tmpl/default.php</filename>
                <filename>tmpl/index.html</filename>

</files>
```

The files section lists all the files from the extension's .zip package that need to be copied onto the server. If you include extra files in the .zip package, but don't list them here, they will get removed when Joomla! cleans up after installing the extension.

For example, the file we will look at next, readme.txt, is not listed in this section. Therefore, it will not get installed on the server, and can only be accessed by unzipping the file locally on our own computer as we did here.

Until recently, building this file list was one of the most frustrating parts of developing and customizing extensions. This is because files often don't get written into the manifest, or, files are written into it but don't get put in the .zip file, causing an error.

The folder element has improved this significantly. This tag allows developers to indicate a folder in the ZIP file, instead of individual files, so that everything inside that folder gets installed.

As an example, if we look at our XML file above we can see there are two files in the tmpl subdirectory. We can replace both of those filename elements with a single folder element like this:

```
<files>

<filename module="mod_fbmodule">mod_fbmodule.php</filename>
 <filename>index.html</filename>
                <filename>helper.php</filename>
<folder>tmpl</folder>

</files>
```

We might also notice that one of the filename tags is a little different than the others:

```
<filename module="mod_fbmodule">mod_fbmodule.php</filename>
```

The `module="mod_fbmodule"` attribute in the tag indicates to Joomla! that the file in this element is the primary file for the extension, and should be called first.

Now there are two exceptions to this rule of entering all files into the manifest.

The first one is the actual XML manifest file itself, which is installed automatically. The other is language files, which have their own tags.

```
<languages>
<language tag="en-GB">en-GB.mod_fbmodule.ini</language>
</languages>
```

The `tag="en-GB"` attribute indicates to Joomla! which language to associate this file with, and should always match the language-locale in the language file name itself.

The last section is the extension parameters is:

```
<params>

<param name="moduleclass_sfx" type="text" default="" label="Module
Class Suffix" description="PARAMMODULECLASSSUFFIX" />

<param name="@spacer" type="spacer" default="" label=""
  description="" />

<param name="user_type" type="list" default="Top" label="TYPE OF USER"
description="DESC OF USER">
<option value="0">Top</option>
<option value="1">Active</option>
</param>

<param name="no_of_users" type="text" default="10" label="NO OF USERS"
description="DESC NO OF USERS"/>

<param name="fb_item_id" type="text" default="2" label="FB ITEM ID"
description="DESC FB ITEM ID"/>

</params>
```

The first parameter is for the module class suffix for this module. This parameter should be included in the parameter for any module we create or customize. However, we don't need to do anything with it. Joomla! will take care of it for us.

 Module class suffixes are used to give individual modules different styling, and will show up automatically on the frontend of your Joomla! site.

After this is a spacer parameter, this does nothing except to draw a line across the parameter form. It is useful for dividing our parameter form up, making it easier to read and understand.

The next three are the parameters specifically for our module. Most of the attributes these three parameters have are fairly easy to understand.

- `name` is the name we will use when retrieving the parameter from within our extension
- `type` indicates the type of parameter, there are many different types, and more information can be found at `http://docs.joomla.org/Standard_parameter_types`
- `default`, as the name suggests, is the default value when the parameter form is loaded for the very first time
- `label` is the text that will be to the left-hand side of the parameter in the parameter screen
- `description` is the text that will be displayed in a pop-up when the user moves their mouse over the label of the parameter

We may notice in the `description` and `label` attributes that there is what looks like a language file Key, for example `description="DESC FB ITEM ID"`. If we look back into our language file, we will see that these are indeed Keys, and will be replaced at run time with the text from the language file.

This useful feature allows us to have our module parameters multi-lingual as well.

Later on, we will remove the `user_type` parameter.

readme.txt

This is the last file in our extension's `.zip` file, and contains a couple of lines of information about the extension. We won't need this when we repackage the file to install on our site so we can just remove it.

So now we have looked at all the files in our module and how they all fit together. The following figure illustrates this operation in a chart:

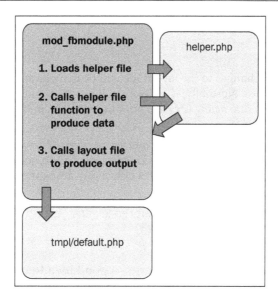

Step 2: Plan out our changes

Now that we understand our module, the next step is to determine what we need to change, and where we need to make the changes.

First, we will decide what we want to change. Then, we will mark out the changes we want to make in our code with comments. Finally, we will work out the code we need to use to make those changes.

"Comments" are notes inside a computer file, which the system does not execute and are only used to communicate information between developers. In PHP, comments can be inserted either by putting `//` at the beginning of a line or `/*` and `*/` around a section of multi-line text. It is also considered a good programming practice to put useful comments into our code.

Decide our changes

The main change we need to make is where the module gets its information from. Currently, it is designed to look for Fireboard forum tables, but we want it to look for Joo!BB tables instead.

We also want to change our layout definition file and make the link on the data in our cells point to Joo!BB.

We will also want to make some changes to our layout file to make it follow correct standards of XHTML.

> Part of our changes to the layout file will be to make some changes to our site's CSS files. Normally, if we were going to distribute an extension, we would create a new CSS file, put our new code in there, and have the extension load it.
>
> However, as we are modifying this for our site only, we don't need to worry about that. Additionally, keeping our CSS in one file will help with our site's performance, even if it's only a tiny amount.

Lastly, we want to remove the `sprintf` references and just output the data directly.

Mark out our changes

Before actually making the changes, it is often a good idea to mark them out with comments. Then, we can go back to put the code in after we have finished all the comments. This is so that we are forced to think through what we are doing from start to finish before we actually start changing things. We can often find important issues we hadn't considered or didn't realize when we first decided to make these changes. If we start writing code without thinking things through, we might not be able to go back easily and correct it.

We will start with the `helper.php` file. Open it up again, and on about line 10 we will see:

```
$query = 'select name,userid, count(userid) as total from #__fb_
messages group by userid order by total desc limit '.$noofusers;
```

Above this code, let's make a comment indicating that we will change this query to look into the Joo!BB tables instead, like so:

```
//TODO-Change this query to get data from Joo!BB tables
$query = 'select name,userid, count(userid) as total from #__fb_
messages group by userid order by total desc limit '.$noofusers;
```

Add the same comment above the other query around line 19.

```
//TODO-Change this query to get data from Joo!BB tables
$query = 'select name,userid,count(userid) as total from (select
name,userid from #__fb_messages order by time desc limit 100) as fb
group by userid order by total desc limit '.$noofusers;
```

Next, open up `tmpl/default.php` and we will add some comments in here to reflect what we plan to do.

To add comments into a layout definition file, we have a couple of choices. Because these files are usually HTML and PHP mixed, we can create PHP blocks just to store our comments or we can use an HTML comment. HTML comments are a little different to PHP ones and can be written like this:

```
<!-- my comment -->
```

We will add some HTML comments to our layout definition file now as shown:

```
<?php defined('_JEXEC') or die('Restricted access'?>

<!--remove this inline CSS and replace with a class -->
<table width="100%" cellpadding="2" cellspacing="2" border=0>

<tr>

<!--remove this inline CSS and replace with a class -->
<!--replace b elements with strong, td with th -->
<td style="text-align:left" width="70%"><b>Member</b></td>
    <td style="text-align:right" width="30%"><b>Posts</b></td>
</tr>

<tr>
<td height="4"></td>
</tr>
<?php foreach ($items as $item) { ?>

<tr>
<!--remove this inline CSS and replace with a class -->
<td style="text-align:left">

<!--edit this link to point to Joo!BB -->
<!--remove sprintf -->
<a href='index.php?option=com_fireboard&func=fbprofile&task=showprf&I
temid=<?php echo $item->fbitemid; ?>&userid=<?php echo $item->userid;
?>'><?php echo JText::sprintf('TOP POSTER', $item->name); ?>
</a>
</td>

<!--remove this inline CSS and replace with a class -->
<!--remove sprintf -->
<td style="text-align:right"><?php echo JText::sprintf('NO OF POSTS',
$item->total); ?>
</td>

</tr>
<?php } ?>
</table>
```

Next up is our main extension file, `mod_fbmodule.php`. Here, we need to remove the references to the `$usertype` parameter, the `if` statement that uses this parameter, and the call to the `getActivePosters` function.

On around line 9 we should see:

```
$usertype = $params->get('user_type');
```

Insert a line above this and add the following comment:

```
//TODO - remove $usertype it is not needed anymore
$usertype = $params->get('user_type');
```

Next, we will look at lines 15 to 19:

```
if ($usertype==0)
{
$items=ModFbModule::getTopPosters($noofusers,$fbitemid);
}else{
$items=ModFbModule::getActivePosters($noofusers,$fbitemid);
}
```

Here, we want to add a comment above all this to say that we need to remove the `if` statement and the `getActivePosters` function call.

```
//TODO - remove the if, else and getActivePosters
if ($usertype==0)
{
$items=ModFbModule::getTopPosters($noofusers,$fbitemid);
}else{
$items=ModFbModule::getActivePosters($noofusers,$fbitemid);
}
```

So now that we have put in all our comments, and we didn't uncover any nasty surprises; we can start writing our code.

Step 3: Make our changes

Now that we have marked out all of our changes, it's time to make them.

helper.php

We will start with our `helper.php` file again. We have to change the query to refer to a different table and different columns to get the data we want.

There are two ways we could do this. We could open up the `.zip` file for the Joo!BB component and try to find where they have their table creating scripts located, or we can just check the database on our site, as we have already installed the component, so just need to look for the tables.

Depending on our setup, we can use either phpMyAdmin, or my preference, the Easy SQL component (mentioned in an earlier chapter as an essential extension for your site) to examine our database.

As I prefer Easy SQL for this sort of job, let's dive in and see what we can find.

The easiest way to start is to open up Easy SQL and just browse the **Table** drop-down list at the top of the screen. Chances are that Joo!BB tables have something in their name that makes them easy to identify.

Sure enough, they all have `joobb` in them as seen here:

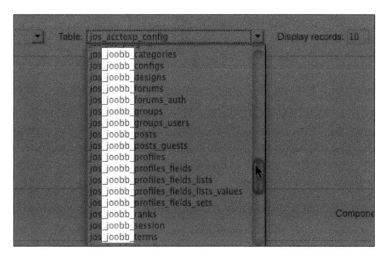

We are looking for user information and we want to sort it by most recent post. Also, by most posts made for our two helper function queries.

First, we need to find the table we are after. If we look through the list of Joo!BB tables, **jos_joobb_posts** looks like our most likely candidate. If we select it from the drop-down list, and press the **Exec SQL** button in the top-right, we will see a list of columns and data currently in the table.

This is definitely information on our posts, so now we want to write some SQL to join to the user table so we can get our user's names, and output the data we want.

Unlike Fireboard, Joo!BB doesn't store any user information in the posts table, only the user id in the `id_user` column. However, we can just join to the regular Joomla! user table and get the user information.

For our most active member, our query needs to do the following:

1. Join the **jos_joobb_posts** table to the **jos_users** table using the user id.
2. Get the username and user id from **jos_users.**
3. Group the records by the user id and count how many posts each one has.
4. Order the output by the totals, in descending order.

This will leave us with a query that looks something like this:

```
SELECT u.username as name,
       u.id as userid,
        count(jp.id) as total
FROM        jos_joobb_posts jp
LEFT JOIN jos_users u
ON jp.id_user = u.id
GROUP BY u.id
ORDER BY total DESC
```

If we put this query into Easy SQL, we should get exactly the output we are after. However, there may be an unnamed record in your list. This is because Joo!BB can allow guests to post (depending on your settings) in the forum, and it is very likely that if we allow guests, then guest will always be our top user. This is because all guests posts will be added together.

So to get around this, we will add a WHERE clause into our SQL to ignore the guest posts.

```
SELECT u.username as name,
       u.id as userid,
        count(jp.id) as total
FROM        jos_joobb_posts jp
LEFT JOIN jos_users u
ON jp.id_user = u.id
WHERE jp.id_user > 0
GROUP BY u.id
ORDER BY total DESC
```

We can just use greater than 0 because all ids apart from guests are positive. This should be a tiny fraction of a second faster than using not equal to.

Now that we have our query, let's put it into our helper file.

Open `helper.php` and we will change lines 10 and 11.

```
$query = 'select name,userid, count(userid) as total from #__fb_
messages group by userid order by total desc limit '.$noofusers;
$db->setQuery($query);
```

Why do we need to change line 11? Because we are going to make a slight adjustment to how this query, and our parameters, are processed. In the original code above, we can see that the variable `$noofusers` is attached to the end of the query as a value for the `LIMIT` clause. This restricts how many records are returned. It is preferable, however, to use the built-in Joomla! functions to apply these limits, so we will change:

```
$db->setQuery($query);
```

into:

```
$db->setQuery($query, 0, $noofusers);
```

which tells the Joomla! database object that we want to start at record `0` (the second parameter) and return `$noofusers` records (the third parameter). This way, we don't need to worry about writing the code in ourselves. Joomla! will take care of it for us.

The final thing we need to do before putting our query in is to change the `jos_` on our table names into `#__` a hash and two underscores.

Why? When we first installed Joomla!, there was a question in the installation about what we want as our database prefix. This prefix is appended to all of our tables, and allows us to have multiple installations of Joomla! using the one database. We are just required to use different database prefixes. Whenever we submit a query to the database via the Joomla! database object, it automatically replaces the `#__` with the appropriate database prefix for our site.

If we hardcode `jos_` into our query, then anyone who doesn't have `jos_` as their database prefix won't be able to use our extension. Even though this extension is only for our site, and we know our prefix is `jos`, it is still preferable for us to follow good programming habits so we remember them in the future.

So the code we should be left with is:

```
$query = 'SELECT u.username as name,
                  u.id as userid,
                    count(jp.id) as total
          FROM    #__joobb_posts jp
```

```
        LEFT JOIN jos_users u
        ON jp.id_user = u.id
        GROUP BY u.id
        ORDER BY total DESC';

$db->setQuery($query, 0, $noofusers);
```

Next, we will cut out our second function `getActivePosters`. To do this, simply delete all the code from lines 24 to 31.

```
public function getActivePosters($noofusers,$fbitemid){

...all the code in between...

}
```

That is it for our helper file.

tmpl/default.php

Now it's time to fix up our layout definition file. We have quite a few changes to make.

The first thing we need to do is decide upon some CSS classes to replace the inline CSS with. A class is a way of grouping and labeling HTML elements and associating them with some CSS. We may also sometimes use an id, which is similar to a class, but should only be used once per page. A class, however, can be used as many times as would like to per page.

The first thing to do is to find elements with the same CSS and then group them together.

Looking over our code we have 5 lines with inline CSS:

```
<table width="100%" cellpadding="2" cellspacing="2" border=0>

<td style="text-align:left" width="70%">
<td style="text-align:right" width="30%">
<td style="text-align:left">
<td style="text-align:right">
```

Even though only the first two `td` elements have a width set, this width will apply to the whole column so it doesn't matter if the width is added to the other `td` elements. Because of this, we can group the `td` element CSS into two classes, one for the right-hand side, and one for the left.

We want to name these two classes something useful so we can see what they do, but also something unique, so that we don't get our classes confused with other ones on the site. This module will display Joo!BB top posters. Since there are two columns, the class names of `jbbTopPostrCol1` and `jbbTopPostrCol2` should work for us. `Col1` can be the left hand side, and `Col2` the right.

Why not call them left and right? Well, when choosing class names, it is better not to choose names that lock us into having that class for a particular style. For example, `textBlue` and `textRed` are not recommended because what happens if we decide that we don't want the text to be blue anymore? We will need to go and change all the `textBlue` references in every single file into `textBrown`, which defeats one of the purposes of using classes in the first place—changing everything in one place.

Better is to call them `textColor1` and `textColor2`, that way if we decide blue isn't right for our site anymore, we can just change the CSS file and not have to rename all our classes.

So for us here, we may want to add a third column to the right-hand side of the other two in the future. What happens then to `jbbTopPostrColRight` if we had named it that? To avoid this dilemma, we will just call them `jbbTopPostrCol1` and `jbbTopPostrCol2`.

We also need a third class for the table itself, which will be - `jbbTopPostrTbl`.

Before we add the classes to our module, and remove the inline CSS, we should add the classes and CSS to our template's CSS file first. Remember, I mentioned above that because we are using this for our site, and not distributing it, we can add these classes to our template's CSS.

So let's open our `template_css.css` file, and add the following to the bottom:

```
.jbbTopPostrTbl {width:100% }
.jbbTopPostrCol1 {text-align:left; width:70%}
.jbbTopPostrCol2 {text-align:right; width:30%}
```

Hang on, why didn't we put in `cellpadding="2" cellspacing="2" border=0` from the table? Because these are not CSS, these are part of the `table` element itself and must be written into the table tags, so we need to leave these for now.

In CSS files, a full stop indicates a class name, and a hash indicates an id. For example:

```
.myClass { ... }
#myID { ... }
```

Now we will upload the `template_css.css` file to our site, and leave it there until we are finished with the module.

Jumping back to `tmpl/default.php`, we can now add the classes to our `table` and `td` elements.

```
<table class="jbbTopPostrTbl" cellpadding="2" cellspacing="2"
border=0>
...
<td class="jbbTopPostrCol1" ><b>Member</b></td>

<td class="jbbTopPostrcol2"><b>Posts</b></td>
...
<td class="jbbTopPostrCol1" >...
<td class="jbbTopPostrCol2" >...
```

Next, we will change the table headers from `td` elements to `th` elements, and change the `b` elements into `strong` elements.

```
<th class="jbbTopPostrCol1" ><strong>Member</strong></th>

<th class="jbbTopPostrcol2"><strong>Posts</strong></th>
```

Now comes an interesting step. We need to change the link on the user's name from a Fireboard profile link to a Joo!BB profile link.

The easiest way to find out what a Joo!BB profile link looks like is to go to our forum and find one. Just look in the right-hand column, where the information about who posted is listed, and click on someone's name as shown in the following screenshot:

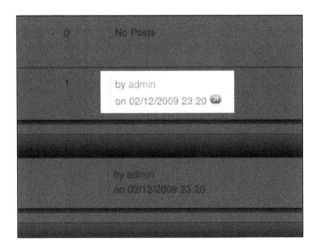

Clicking the link on our site should give us a URL of something like:

```
http://www.mysite.com/component/option,com_joobb/Itemid,53/id,62/
view,profile/
```

This URL has been changed by our SEF links component, to make it a little more user-friendly. However, we need to break it down into the real link by replacing the slashes with ampersands, the commas with equals signs, and the word component with ?index.php.

This leaves us with the following URL:

```
http:// www.mysite.com?index.php&option=com_joobb&Itemid=53&id=62&
view=profile
```

When adding a URL to an extension, we should run it through a function in the JRoute class. This will allow for SEF components to properly reformat our URL before it appears on the site.

Because JRoute is a PHP class we will need to add some extra PHP code to our layout definition.

Change this:

```php
<?php foreach ($items as $item) { ?>
```

into this:

```php
<?php foreach ($items as $item) {

$profileLink = JRoute::_('http:// www.mysite.com?index.php&option=com_
joobb&Itemid='.$item->fbitemid.'&id='.$item->userid.'&view=profile');

?>
```

We are now building the link in PHP, which includes adding in our item id and user id, then putting it all through the JRoute::_() function.

Because our link is now built in the PHP section of our file, we need to change the link code lower down.

We can now change our long URL:

```html
<td class="jbbTopPostrColl" >

<a href='index.php?option=com_fireboard&func=fbprofile&task=showprf&I
temid=<?php echo $item->fbitemid; ?>&userid=<?php echo $item->userid;
?>'><?php echo JText::sprintf('TOP POSTER', $item->name); ?></a>

</td>
```

Into one that is much shorter:

```
<td class="jbbTopPostrCol1" >

<a href='<?php echo $profileLink; ?>'><?php echo JText::sprintf('TOP
  POSTER', $item->name); ?></a>

</td>
```

Let's make it even shorter by removing all the `sprintf` references:

```
<td class="jbbTopPostrCol1" >

<a href='<?php echo $profileLink; ?>'><?php echo $item->name; ?></a>

</td>
```

Also our other column:

```
<td class="jbbTopPostrCol2" >

<?php echo $item->total; ?>

</td>
```

And with that, our layout definition is complete.

mod_fbmodule.php

We are almost complete. Just two more files to change. The first one is our primary extension file, mod_fbmodule.php.

This one is very simple as it is just deleting unwanted code that we indicated with our comments before. We will remove the lines marked as follows:

```
$params->get('user_type');
$noofusers = $params->get('no_of_users');
$fbitemid = $params->get('fb_item_id');

if ($usertype==0) {

$items = ModFbModule::getTopPosters($noofusers,$fbitemid);

}else{

$items=ModFbModule::getActivePosters($noofusers,$fbitemid);

}
```

That's it!

mod_fbmodule.xml

The last file we need to change is the XML manifest.

This is, again, an easy job for us. We will just remove the lines marked below, which define the parameter for the type of display. We are no longer using that parameter, so it is best that we remove it.

```
<params>

<param name="moduleclass_sfx" type="text" default="" label="Module
Class Suffix" description="PARAMMODULECLASSSUFFIX" />

<param name="@spacer" type="spacer" default="" label="" description=""
/>

<param name="user_type" type="list" default="Top" label="TYPE OF USER"
description="DESC OF USER">
<option value="0">Top</option>
<option value="1">Active</option>
</param>

<param name="no_of_users" type="text" default="10" label="NO OF USERS"
description="DESC NO OF USERS"/>

<param name="fb_item_id" type="text" default="2" label="FB ITEM ID"
description="DESC FB ITEM ID"/>

</params>
```

With that, we should be done.

Step 4: Install and test our module

Now all that is left is to install and test our module.

1. Compress all of our files up into a .zip file.

2. Install our module the same way we would in any other extension.

3. Click on **Extensions | Module Manager** and find our module.

  Newly installed modules always appear at the bottom of the left module position modules.

Now, enter in our parameters, and make sure that our module is enabled. Refresh our site. We should now see the same thing as shown in the following illustration:

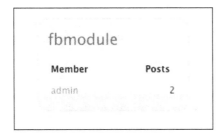

Congratulations on a successful customization! From here we could tweak the CSS, change the module name to something useful, and get some more people posting in our forums so that our list fills up.

Summary

We have now finished a successful module customization, and improved a lot of the code as well. We also looked at how modules operate, and at module in a module execution.

Next, we will look at plug-ins and what they can do to help our site.

7
Customizing Plugins

Plugins are an essential, but rarely noticed part of a successful Joomla!-based business. I say rarely noticed because they usually operate unseen in the background unlike modules and components whose output is obvious and noticeable.

Plugins are very flexible and can execute for various purposes at many different times. Part of this chapter will be to look at these purposes and times, and understand how they can affect our web site by going through the following topics:

- plugin composition and operation
- plugin types
- plugin events
- plugin ordering
- plugin customization

We will also make some changes to an existing plugin so that it better meets our needs.

Plugin composition and operation

Like a module, in its simplest form, a plugin can consist of only two files, a PHP file with the actual code for the plugin, and an XML manifest that tells Joomla! what to do with the plugin.

Despite this apparent simplicity, plugins are very powerful, and more difficult to understand than modules and components.

Plugins are designed to run at certain times during the execution of our site, and they perform actions that can only be done at these times.

For example, in our sample site we want to hide some of our content from guests, and only show it to paid subscribers. This action can only be performed when we are actually preparing the content to be displayed, because we need to wait until we identify if the viewer is a guest or subscriber, and then make the changes to the content dynamically.

In a different example, checking if a subscriber's subscription is valid is something that only needs to be done when they try to login, and not on every page load.

Plugin types

Plugins are divided into eight types, as follows:

- Authentication
- Content
- Editors
- Editors-XTD
- Search
- System
- User
- XML-RPC

Authentication

Authentication plugins are designed to allow the site to check the user's authentication against a variety of sources.

The default is to check the user's authentication against a username and password stored in the Joomla! database, which, as of Joomla! 1.5, will be the username and password fields in the #__user table (#__ is the table prefix we chose when setting up Joomla!). However, any source with a public API can be used to verify someone's authentication details.

Common uses are LDAP, OpenID, a Google account, a subscription, community component, and more.

On our site, for example, we are already using an authentication plugin to verify the subscriptions of users when they attempt to login.

Content

Possibly the most commonly used of all plugins, content plugins allow content items to be modified or have additional features added to them.

We could, for example, use content plugins to cloak email addresses, embed audio or video into our pages, or do text replacements. We can even embed components and modules into our pages via plugins.

We will later look at a content plugin that we will use to hide and show content depending on a user's subscription.

Editors

Editors plugins add WYSIWYG editors that we can use when editing our content.

We installed JCE on our site earlier, which is the most popular Joomla! editor plugin as of this publication according to `Joomla.org`.

Editors-XTD

Editors-XTD (extended) plugins allow us to add additional buttons to the editors. The **Image**, **Read more**, and **Pagebreak** buttons on the default Joomla! WYSIWYG editor, for example, are actually plugins.

Search

Search plugins allow us to search through the data from different components.

By default, Joomla! comes with plugins that search through content articles and the Contacts and Weblinks components. These can be expanded upon by creating or installing search plugins for other extensions.

System

System plugins are arguably the most powerful and most flexible types of plugins for Joomla!, as they can execute at several different pre-defined points during the execution of a Joomla! page plugin.

They can be used to perform a vast array of functions, such as loading extra scripts or CSS into the header of a web page, redirecting people away from pages, logging statistics, and more.

User

User plugins allow us to perform actions at different times with respect to users. Such times include logging in and out, and also when saving changes to a user's profile. User plugins are often used to create a "bridge" between Joomla! and other web applications (such as the phpBB forum or the osCommerce e-commerce platform.).

XML-RPC

XML-RPC plugins are for communicating between our Joomla! site and other external applications, such as a desktop application or a different web site.

Plugin events

As a Joomla! site loads a page, it steps through a series of events as part of that process. The events it steps through are determined by the type of page it is loading. Plugins are always tied to one or more of these events, and are executed during those events as required.

When loading a page of content, for example, we would step through a mix of the system and some of the content events. When loading the same page for editing, we will step through the system events, different content events, and also possibly editor events.

The events triggered in Joomla! are:

Authentication

- onAuthenticate

Content

- onPrepareContent
- onAfterDisplayTitle
- onBeforeDisplayContent
- onBeforeContentSave
- onAfterContentSave

Editors

- onInit
- onGetContent
- onSetContent

- onSave
- onDisplay
- onGetInsertMethod

Editors XTD (Extended)

- onDisplay

Search

- onSearch
- onSearchAreas

System

- onAfterInitialise
- onAfterRoute
- onAfterDispatch
- onAfterRender

User

- onLoginUser
- onLoginFailure
- onLogoutUser
- onLogoutFailure
- onBeforeStoreUser
- onAfterStoreUser
- onBeforeDeleteUser
- onAfterDeleteUser

XML-RPC

- onGetWebServices

Most of these events are easy to understand from their name, but just in case, more information can be found on the Joomla! documentation wiki at http://docs.joomla.org/CategoryPlugins.

Some events are only activated at specific times, such as onAuthenticate, which is only activated when someone logs into their account. Others are activated on every page load. Content events are activated on all content pages and only on content pages, not on pages with components other than com_content.

Content plugins are also only executed on the main body content itself and don't have access to the template or other module data. So a text replacement content plugin, for example, wouldn't change any text in modules or the template, only in the main content itself.

 It is actually possible for modules and components to manually activate plugin events with clever programming, but this is not the default Joomla! behavior. It is usually done when a developer wants to apply content plugin restrictions/changes to a module.

Plugin order

Aside from the events and types, there is a third important factor to consider when setting up our plugins. That is the order in which the plugins of a particular type are executed. This order is best observed on the **Plugin Manager** screen that can be found under the **Extensions** menu.

The order in which the plugins execute is something not many people think about, but is really quite powerful and useful. This is because the plugins which execute later, can then use the output or effects of the earlier executing plugins as input.

For example, imagine we have a plugin that displays different text for different user types, and we have another plugin that reads certain text values and replaces them with embedded video or audio. If we wanted to be able to show different videos to different groups, then we could use the first plugin to generate the different command strings for the second plugin, and have it generate them based on the user type.

The second plugin, our media embedding plugin, doesn't even know that the first plugin exists. All it knows is which videos it needs to display based on what is in the content item.

If the media plugin executes first, then it will generate both videos regardless of the user type.

As another example, imagine we have some sort of external application and we log users into it after they authenticate via an authentication plugin. We need to make sure that this plugin is executed after all of our other authentication plugins that may check a user's credentials or account status. Otherwise, someone may get logged into our external application even though they were prevented from login into our Joomla! site. So a hacker, for example, could get access to our external application without needing to even successfully get into our main site. This was all because we had the order of our plugins wrong.

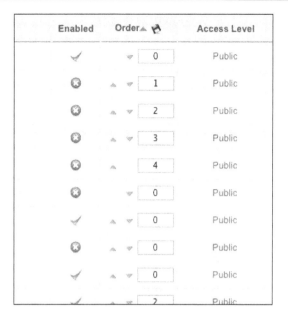

So when we install and activate plugins, it is well worth taking the time to double check that everything happens in the order it is meant to be in. If one of our plugins is not behaving how it should, it might be worth checking the order to see if another plugin is conflicting with it.

Customizing a Plugin

Now that we have a better understanding of how our plugins work and fit together, we are going to try our hand at customizing one for our site. This will hopefully give us the understanding and confidence to make any other customizations we need in the future.

As with modules, it is often easier to find a plugin that does most of what we want it to do and then make changes to it so that it meets our needs more completely.

Looking back over our goals, one that requires a plugin is that we want to limit access to certain parts of our content to only our paying subscribers. This effect is going to be best achieved via content plugin, so we chose the Ninja Access plugin to fill this need.

To use Ninja Access we first need to mark the content we want to restrict with special tags and indicate the user groups we want to see what is contained within the tags. When the page is produced, the plugin reads the visitor's user group and then compares it to the ones in the list provided by the tag.

If the user groups match, then the content is displayed, if not, then it is hidden.

For example:

```
{njaccess 0}shows only to guest users{/njaccess}
{njaccess 18,19,20,21,23,24,25}shows to all users who are not a
guest{/njaccess}
```

The numbers in the examples above indicate the default Joomla! user group ids.

The most important ones are:

- 0 = Guests
- 18 = Registered
- 24 = Administrators
- 25 = Super Administrators

We could use this as it is, but as we don't have a component installed to create new access groups, it won't be very flexible. We could get into trouble in the future if we decide to let people register without getting a subscription, or create a free subscription. In this instance, we will have paying and free subscribers all in the number 18 user group.

Also, as we are always going to be restricting the same groups, we don't really need to type the parameters in every single time. Making our plugins always restrict the same groups automatically will save us some time and reduce mistakes.

Lastly, do we really need to type njaccess every time? Let's shorten it to something like soc—subscriber only content.

For our first dilemma, a better idea than groups might be to associate the access to certain AEC subscriptions that are currently active. That way if people's subscriptions expire, or they get a free account, the content is still properly controlled regardless of their user groups.

Step 1: Understand the existing code

The customizing process for plugins is basically identical to modules. We will start by unzipping the file that the plugin came in, plg_ninjaaccess_v1.1.zip. Now, let's take a look at the ZIP file's contents.

en-GB.plg_content_njaccess.ini

This should now be easily recognizable as a language file, after working with one in the previous chapter. We can see that the name is slightly different but the convention is the same, `<language>-<locale>.<extension_name>.ini`.

Opening up this file, we find a single line:

```
NINJACONTENT=<IFRAME SRC="../plugins/content/njaccess/njaccess_desc.
html" WIDTH=600 HEIGHT=600 FRAMEBORDER=0 SCROLLING=yes></IFRAME>
```

This doesn't look much like a typical language entry. After the Key, the Value is actually some HTML calling an IFrame.

This is actually a work around for a "bug" in the current (current at time of writing) Joomla! code that handles modules and plugins.

Description handling in Joomla! Plugins and modules

In Joomla! 1.0, rich extension descriptions, descriptions containing HTML, links, images, detailed information and instructions, and so on were usually done by wrapping everything in CDATA tags in the XML manifest. However, with Joomla! 1.5, a move was made to allow for greater language support, and developers were encouraged to use the new .ini style language files instead of CDATA to display their descriptions.

This did make sense, and has allowed for greater language support. However, left developers (like myself) who liked having rich extension descriptions with a bit of a problem. The problem was that .ini language files need to contain the entire Value for a certain Key on a single line. So what would usually be 200-500 lines of HTML and data was now compressed down to one line. This made finding and fixing problems, or editing the description pages, very difficult.

To top it off, when we install a module or plugin for the first time the language files aren't actually loaded, so all we see is the Key value. It isn't until we go to the parameters screen that we see the language file contents.

Conversely, CDATA works in the install screen, but not in the parameters screen for a module or plugin.

As an answer to this, some developers decided to use IFrames that called an external file, which was formatted with the description information, until a more suitable solution can be found.

Our custom Plugin description

Lucky that we do not need to worry about a fancy description page because this will be our private custom plugin and we don't need to teach others how to use it. Normally, we could just remove this here, but with our custom plugin we may want it to output a message for our visitors when content is explaining to them that they can see it if they get a subscription. So for now we will leave this file as it is and edit it later.

njaccess.php

This is the main part of our plugin, and where we will do most of our work.

Let's take a look at the code piece by piece.

```
defined('_JEXEC') or die( "Direct Access Is Not Allowed" );

jimport('joomla.eventPlugin');
```

The first line is our ever-important check to make sure that our code is running inside a Joomla! site. If this line is ever missing from some code it is a potential security risk, so we need to always include it if it is missing. It cannot be stressed enough how important this check is.

Next, we load the plugin event class, which gives us access to the JPlugin class, which we will use as shown:

```
class plgContentNJaccess extends JPlugin {

    function plgContentNJaccess ( &$subject ) {
            parent::__construct( $subject );
            $this->_plugin = JPluginHelper::getPlugin('Content',
                                                    'ninjaacess');
            $this->_params = new JParameter($this->_plugin->params);
    }
```

Now we start the main part of our plugin, which is our plugin class, plgContentNJaccess. The name is comprised of three parts:

- plg, identifying this as a plugin
- Content, indicating the type of plugin this is—a content plugin
- Njaccess, the name of our plugin file, without the .php

This is a very important naming convention used for plugins and needs to be followed if we want to make use of the Joomla! framework functions. The convention is:

`plg` + proper case name of the plugin type + proper case name of the plugin file without the extension.

Proper case means that we capitalize the first letter of each word when we assemble them. Once assembled, it's then referred to as "Camel Case", which is a reference to how the capital letters in the one word look like humps on a camel. Strictly speaking, the case is not actually important for execution as PHP classes are not case-sensitive but it's the convention Joomla! uses and does make the code easier to read.

Our plugin class is created as an extension of the `JPlugin` class. What this does is allow our class to inherit all the functions and variables of the `JPlugin` class, which we need for the basic running of a plugin, and so we can add our own to it for the extra functionality we want.

 Some of the terminology used here is specific to a style of programming known as Object-oriented Design. For more information, see
`http://en.wikipedia.org/wiki/Object-oriented_design`.

After our class statement we have a function called `plgContentNJaccess`. We may notice that this is the same name as our class. This is because this first function is what is called a 'constructor' function, and gets executed when the class is loaded. This is a great place to do any preparation we need for running our plugin. In this case, Ninja Access is loading the parameters for itself via the lines:

```
$this->_plugin = JPluginHelper::getPlugin( 'Content', 'njaccess' );

$this->_params = new JParameter( $this->_plugin->params );
```

The first line loads all the information Joomla! has stored for our content type plugin named `njaccess`. Then, we convert the flat data that is stored in the Joomla! `params` column into a parameter object which is then stored in `_params` (note the underscore).

After our constructor function is another function.

```
function onPrepareContent(&$article, &$params, $limitstart)
{
$regex = "#{njaccess(.*?)}(.*?){/njaccess}#s";

$article->text = preg_replace_callback($regex,array($this,"njaccess"),
  $article->text);

return true;

}
```

Now this is looking a little more complex than our module from the previous chapter.

First, let's look at the name of this function — onPrepareContent. That looks familiar doesn't it? Where did we see that before? Well, it looks familiar because it's the same name as one of our content plugin events.

One Joomla! plugin can actually contain multiple events, as long as they are for the same plugin type. The way we tell Joomla! which function to execute when is via the function name. In this case, we want to check our code and replace the values while we are preparing the content. This is always the best event if we want to alter the contents of a content item.

The onPrepareContent function receives three parameters:

- $article, which is the contents of our content item
- $params, which is the parameter settings for the content item
- $limitstart, which is the number of the page of the content item (if multipage)

From these parameters, we can then start to modify our content item.

The next line is a bit confusing. What exactly does regex mean, and what is the crazy piece of text being assigned to it?

```
$regex = "#{njaccess(.*?)}(.*?){/njaccess}#s";
```

Well, regex stands for **regular expression**, which is a system for searching for patterns in blocks of text. The crazy piece of text is the pattern we are going to be searching for.

There are many different symbols and patterns we can use for a regex, but the one we are using here is relatively simple, the # and #s on either end indicate that we will ignore anything on either side of our search pattern (except for other copies of the pattern of course). The {njaccess is actually the real text that we are searching for.

The next piece of the regex is special, (.*?). This indicates that we want to collect everything between the real texts on either side, and do something with it. It will be put into an array with all the values we collect. For the Ninja Access plugin, the data in here will be the list of user group ids that are allowed to see the content between the tags.

Just after these collector symbols is another single character of real text, a closing brace, }, which closes our {njaccess tag we opened earlier.

After this, we have another patch of collector symbols. These are collecting the actual text that we want to show/hide. This text will be put into the same array as the first set of collected data.

Then finally, we have a closing tag, {njaccess}, which finishes our pattern off.

 There are a lot of sites around the web where we can learn more about different regex patterns and how to write them ourselves. We can just put the word "regex" into our favorite search engine to find them.

The next line down is where the magic begins.

```
$article->text = preg_replace_callback($regex,array($this,"njaccess"),
    $article->text);
```

We take the $article parameter which was passed in, and we are going to assign a new value to its text attribute. The text attribute is where the actual contents of our content item are.

Then we call a function, preg_replace_callback. This function is used to perform regex searches and then, it will execute a function for every instance of the search pattern it finds.

The three parameters we are using for this function are first, a regular expression search pattern, in this case $regex that we made earlier.

The next one is a function to execute, or an array containing an object, and the name of a member function within that object to execute. We are choosing the second route, choosing the object member function, and passing it our plgContentNJaccess class via the $this variable, and telling it to call the njaccess function, which we will look at in a moment.

 An array is a type of variable that holds multiple separate values within itself. Arrays are usually used to hold lists of related data, such as a list of staff id or names. Arrays are referenced by using the notation $arrayName[arrayId]. The array id is usually a number and is the method used to pick out individual pieces of data. More information can be found here: www.php.net/array.

The third parameter is the text we want to search through. In this case, we are going to pass the text attribute of our $article object.

The final line in our function returns the output from our `preg_replace_callback` function, which should now contain our edited text.

Now, we have the final function for our `plgContentNJaccess` class, and the function we called in the parameters for `preg_replace_callback`.

```
function njaccess(&$matches)
{
$user           = &JFactory::getUser();
$acl            = &JFactory::getACL();

$myRealGid = intval( $acl->get_group_id( $user->usertype ) );
$accessLevels = '';

$output= $matches[2];

if (@$matches[1])
{
$accessLevels = explode(",", trim($matches[1]));
}

if (in_array($myRealGid,$accessLevels))
return $output;

return "";

}
```

Here we have named the function `njaccess` for consistency. Since this is an internal function for our class, we could have called it anything we wanted. In fact, it might have been better to call it `textReplace` or something similar.

The first thing we need to notice is the parameter that our function receives. The only one coming in is the `$matches` variable, which is an array containing in position 0 the complete matched string, and in positions 1 and above, all the values that we collected with our collection patterns. We only have two collection patterns, so our `$matches` array will only have positions 0, 1, and 2 populated.

Position 1 will have our list of user groups, and position 2 our text that we want to show/hide.

Our function begins with us calling in the ACL (user groups) and user information and putting them into two variables.

```
$user           = &JFactory::getUser();
$acl            = &JFactory::getACL();

$myRealGid = intval( $acl->get_group_id( $user->usertype ) );
```

The $user variable contains the output from JFactory::getUser(), which will be a user object filled with information about the visitor for whom this actual page is being generated.

We then use this user's information and find out their user group so we can compare it later on.

```
$accessLevels = '';
```

This next line just creates an empty variable. PHP can throw error and warning messages if we try to print out a variable that hasn't been created. The $accessLevels variable may not actually get populated or created later on, so we will create it here and make it empty to avoid notices or errors.

```
$output= $matches[2];
```

Next, we take the position 2 data from our $matches array, which is our text we want to show/hide, and put it into $output. This isn't really needed, but is just to make it easier to handle and understand instead of writing $matches[2] all the time.

```
if (@$matches[1])
{
$accessLevels = explode(",", trim($matches[1]));
}
```

This next section says if we have a value in $matches[1] our list of user groups then we will explode the data and put it into our $accessLevels variable.

What does explode mean? It is a PHP function that takes a list of values that are delimited (separated) by a certain string of values, breaks them up according to that string, and puts them into an array.

For example, in this case we are taking a list of comma separated values and splitting them up by the comma, removing the comma in the process (so be careful with this), and then placing each of the broken up strings into positions in an array.

So the string "18,24,25" would become an array like this:

- Position 0 => 18
- Position 1 => 24
- Position 2 -> 25

Why are we putting them into an array?

```
if (in_array($myRealGid,$accessLevels))
return $output;
```

This is why. We can now use the `in_array` function to compare our page visitor's group id to the array of group ids that are allowed to see this information. If there is a match, then we return `$output`, which contains our text.

Whenever the command `return` is executed from within a function, that function immediately stops operating and doesn't execute any more code in the function unless it is called again. It also passes back whatever value (if any) is specified after the `return` keyword.

If there is no match between our visitor's group id, and the group ids allowed to see this text, then we skip the next line, `return $output`, and continue executing, which gets us to the final line:

```
return "";
```

This line tells our function to end and returns an empty string, effectively hiding our text.

njaccess.xml

Again, as with our module, this file is our XML manifest and contains the information that Joomla! needs to put our plugin in the right place and to get it operating properly.

```xml
<?xml version="1.0" encoding="utf-8"?>
<install version="1.5" type="plugin" group="content">
<name>Ninja Access</name>
<author>Daniel Chapman</author>
<creationDate>February 2008</creationDate>
<copyright>(C) 2008 Ninja Forge</copyright>
    <license>http://www.gnu.org/copyleft/gpl.html GNU/GPL</license>
    <authorEmail>daniel@ninjaforge.com</authorEmail>
    <authorUrl>www.ninjaforge.com</authorUrl>
    <version>1.1</version>
    <description>NINJACONTENT</description>
<files>
<filename plugin="njaccess">njaccess.php</filename>
        <filename>njaccess/njaccess_desc.html</filename>
        <filename>njaccess/js/ninja.js</filename>
          <filename>njaccess/images/logo.jpg</filename>
          <filename>njaccess/images/ninjoomla.png</filename>
          <filename>njaccess/images/firefox2.gif</filename>
          <filename>njaccess/images/jcda.png</filename>
          <filename>njaccess/images/validation_xhtml.png</filename>
          <filename>njaccess/images/validation_css.png</filename>
          <filename>njaccess/images/info.png</filename>
          <filename>njaccess/images/change.png</filename>
          <filename>njaccess/images/inst.png</filename>
```

```
        <filename>njaccess/images/tabbg.gif</filename>
        <filename>njaccess/images/tab2.png</filename>
        <filename>njaccess/images/gnugpl.png</filename>
</files>
<params>
</params>
<languages>
<language tag="en-GB">en-GB.plg_content_njaccess.ini</language>
</languages>
</install>
```

There is quite a lot in here, but we should be familiar with most of it by now.

The most important parts for us now are the lines that are unique to plugins. Lines such as:

```
<install version="1.5" type="plugin" group="content">
```

In the last chapter, our module's XML manifest read:

```
<install type="module" version="1.5.0">
```

Essentially they are the same, except that the plugin has one extra attribute in the `install` tag, a `group` attribute. This attribute, as we can probably guess, identifies the type of plugin this is, content, system, authentication, and so on.

We will also notice that our description tags have a language file Key in them:

```
<description>NINJACONTENT</description>
```

The Value for this Key loads an external HTML file in an IFrame instead of being actual text as we saw earlier.

Looking at the list of files we can also see a line that is similar, but slightly different than our module.

```
<filename plugin="njaccess">njaccess.php</filename>
```

In our module we had:

```
<filename module="mod_fbmodule">mod_fbmodule.php</filename>
```

Based on what we know about the module, we should be able to work out what this does. That's right, it identifies to Joomla! that this particular file is the main file for the plugin and should be executed first.

The rest?

Looking at the rest of our file list, there are a lot of files that we haven't looked at yet, particularly the many image files. These files are all for the rich description, and used in the IFrame our language file loads. We will remove these later to streamline our plugin since as we don't need it for our own plugin.

Step 2: Plan out our changes

Just like with our module, we are going to be systematic about our customization. This keeps us organized and reduces the chances for mistakes.

Really, these changes are so simple we could probably just dive in and do them, but we want to build good habits for when we want to customize more complex extensions.

Step 2.1: Decide on our changes

Our plugin is going to be essentially the same, hiding or showing parts of our content depending on a particular condition. Only we want to change it so the condition we use is user's subscription and not their user group. We will need to put in some code to search the database for the visitor's subscription information.

We also want to clean out any code we don't need, such as the description HTML page and images.

In our module from the last chapter, we left most things pretty much as they were, only renaming things if we needed to. This time, we will go a little bit further and rename our extension and functions. One day we may want to distribute this plugin to get some traffic to our site, and help other developers like ourselves.

Also, seeing as we are going to rebuild most of this plugin, let's put a short description in to remind us what it is for, or in case we hire another developer to help with our site later, they can see what it does.

Step 2.2: Mark out our changes

Remember that before we actually make our changes, we want to go through the code and mark them with comments first. This way we are forced to think the whole process through from start to finish before we write any code, and we can see any potential problems before they happen. This beats finding them after we have spent a few hours writing code, and wasting that time going back to repair them.

en-GB.plg_content_njaccess.ini

First, we are going to edit our language file, `en-GB.plg_content_njaccess.ini`.

 If we were making a complex component, we would usually keep the language file open the entire time, and add new entries to it every time we wanted to put some text onto the screen. But our plugin is pretty much a 'behind the scenes' plugin so we don't need much text.

So what text do we need?

Well, as we discussed above, when we hide some content from a user, we probably want to display a message that tells them that it has been hidden, and that they should get a subscription to read it. We also want to remove the current rich description and replace it with simpler, normal text.

So let's add a note to our current code,

```
NINJACONTENT=<IFRAME SRC="../plugins/content/njaccess/njaccess_desc.
html" WIDTH=600 HEIGHT=600 FRAMEBORDER=0 SCROLLING=yes></IFRAME>
```

that tells us to delete it completely. Then we will add a note to write our description and message in its place.

```
# TODO-Remove this
NINJACONTENT=<IFRAME SRC="../plugins/content/njaccess/njaccess_desc.
html" WIDTH=600 HEIGHT=600 FRAMEBORDER=0 SCROLLING=yes></IFRAME>

# TODO-Add plain text description
# TODO-Add message for hidden text
```

Wait a minute! What are these hashes? We haven't seen them before. Up until now we were told that comments were either double slashes (`//`), enclosing slash asterisks (`/* ... */`), or for HTML some long tags (`<!-- ... -->`).

Well, `.ini` files are different from our `.php` files, and are processed differently. As a result, they use a different symbol to indicate for comments. So now, we can add `#` to our list of comment symbols, but for `.ini` (language) files only.

njaccess.php

Next, open up `njaccess.php`. As we are basically re-writing this plugin, we might as well change the name of this file and all the functions to something more relevant.

```
// TODO-Rename this file

// Ensure this file is being included by a parent file. defined('_
JEXEC') or die( "Direct Access Is Not Allowed" );
```

```
jimport('joomla.eventplugin');

// TODO- Rename the class to match our new filename
class plgContentNJaccess extends JPlugin {

// TODO- Rename this constructor
function plgContentNJaccess( &$subject )
{...
```

We don't have any parameters, so we can remove the parameter loading from the constructor.

```
...
parent::__construct( $subject );
// TODO-
Remove these as we have no need for parameters
$this->_plugin = JPluginHelper::getPlugin( 'Content',
                                            'ninjaaccess' );

$this->_params = new JParameter( $this->_plugin->params );

}
```

We are renaming everything, so we should rename our `regex` tags and the function call via `preg_replace_callback` as well.

```
function onPrepareContent(&$article, &$params, $limitstart) {
// TODO- Adjust our regex to look for a shorter tag
//      and one collector function between the tags
$regex = "#{njaccess(.*?)}(.*?){/njaccess}#s";

// TODO- Rename the function call
$article->text = preg_replace_callback($regex,array($this,"njaccess"),
$article->text);
return true;

}

// TODO- Rename the function
function njaccess(&$matches) {
```

We also want to remove any references to the ACL. We do want to continue to load the user information though, as we need their user id (if logged in) to compare it to the subscriptions in the AEC tables.

```
$user        = &JFactory::getUser();

// TODO- Remove the next 3 lines as we don't need ACL
$acl         = &JFactory::getACL();

$myRealGid = intval( $acl->get_group_id( $user->usertype ) );

$accessLevels = '';
```

We are only going to have one collector pattern now, so only one set of information, the text to be shown/hidden, needs to be collected. To do this, we need to change all the references to $matches[2] into $matches[1] and remove the old $matches[1] checks.

```
// TODO-change this to matches[1] as we only have
//        one collector now
$output= $matches[2];

// TODO-Remove this
if (@$matches[1]) {

$accessLevels = explode(",", trim($matches[1]));

}
```

Lastly, we need to replace the main processing with a query to check our visitor's user id against the AEC subscription tables for an active paying subscription.

```
// TODO-Replace this with a query searching for the
//        user's id in the subscriptions table, searching
//        for a paying subscription
if (in_array($myRealGid,$accessLevels))
return $output;

// TODO- Get the visitor's id if available.
//        If a guest (id = 0) then skip this and display
//        the please subscribe message

// TODO- Look for the id in the AEC subscriptions
//        table, and check if they have a valid, paid
//        subscription. If so, return the text
//        if not, skip it and return the message

// TODO- Instead of blank, return our message from our
//        language file
return "";

}

}
```

njaccess.xml

Finally, we come to our `njaccess.xml` file. Comments can be made into XML files in the same way as HTML `<!-- ... -->`.

For our XML manifest, we have a few things to do. At first, we want to rename everything from `njaccess`, including the manifest itself.

```
<?xml version="1.0" encoding="utf-8"?>
<install version="1.5" type="plugin" group="content">
<!-- TODO- Rename this file and plugin -->
<name>Ninja Access</name>
<author>Daniel Chapman</author>
<creationDate>February 2008</creationDate>
<copyright>(C) 2008 Ninja Forge</copyright>
    <license>http://www.gnu.org/copyleft/gpl.html GNU/GPL</license>
    <authorEmail>daniel@ninjaforge.com</authorEmail>
    <authorUrl>www.ninjaforge.com</authorUrl>
```

Also, let's change the version number of our new plugin to 1.0. Then change the description as well, to suit what we put into our language file.

```
<!-- TODO- Change to 1.0 -->
<version>1.1</version>
<!-- TODO- Change to match our language file -->
<description>NINJACONTENT</description>
```

Then, we want to remove all the unnecessary files from the description

```
<!-- TODO- Remove unneeded files -->
<files>
<filename plugin="njaccess">njaccess.php</filename>
        <filename>njaccess/njaccess_desc.html</filename>
        <filename>njaccess/js/ninja.js</filename>
          <filename>njaccess/images/logo.jpg</filename>
          <filename>njaccess/images/ninjoomla.png</filename>
          <filename>njaccess/images/firefox2.gif</filename>
          <filename>njaccess/images/jcda.png</filename>
          <filename>njaccess/images/validation_xhtml.png</filename>
          <filename>njaccess/images/validation_css.png</filename>
          <filename>njaccess/images/info.png</filename>
          <filename>njaccess/images/change.png</filename>
          <filename>njaccess/images/inst.png</filename>
          <filename>njaccess/images/tabbg.gif</filename>
          <filename>njaccess/images/tab2.png</filename>
          <filename>njaccess/images/gnugpl.png</filename>
</files>
```

Finally, rename the reference to our language file to suit the new filename:

```
<params>
</params>
<!-- TODO- Rename the language file -->
<languages>
<language tag="en-GB">en-GB.plg_content_njaccess.ini</language>
</languages>
</install>
```

Step 3: Make our changes

Now comes the big moment of putting in our actual changes.

Before we do anything, we need to make a decision. We said we are going to rename everything, but to what?

Well, what is our plugin going to do? It hides text based on AEC subscriptions. Keeping this in mind, we should think of a name that captures that as much as possible so we can recognize our plugin easily.

Something like this really comes down to personal choice, but generally we want to keep it around the 10-15 characters mark. Too many characters and it starts to make things like filenames and class names too long to be useful.

We are going to go with AEC Subscription Hider, abbreviated aecsubshider. It's informative enough to give us an idea of what it does, but not so long that we get lost reading it.

The very first thing we will do now is rename and remove our files.

To get rid of the rich description files is quite easy. Just remove the entire `njaccess` folder.

Next, we need to rename the remaining three files, `njaccess.xml`, `njaccess.php`, and `en-GB.plg_content_njaccess.ini`. So edit the file names by changing them to the following:

- `aecsubshider.xml`
- `aecsubshider.php`
- `en-GB.plg_content_aecsubshider.ini`

Now let's fix the internals of our files.

en-GB.plg_content_aecsubshider.ini

Let's just follow our own comments here and remove the old Ninja Access description, replace it with one of our own, and add a message for people to get a subscription. In the end, our language file should look like this:

```
# Plain text description
AECSUBSHIDER DESC=This plugin hides or shows text based on whether the
visitor has an active AEC subscription or not.

# Message for hidden text
HIDDEN=The next portion of this article is for paying subscribers
only. Please become a member to view it.
```

Notice that we left part of our comments in there this time? This is to help us, or another developer, in the future if we want to edit this file. Leaving the comments leaves us hints on what each piece of text is for.

aecsubshider.php

First, let's remove and rename all our marked code. We can also remove the comments for these too as we don't need to be reminded of the code we removed or renamed.

We will handle our `regex` tag a bit differently, so leave it for now.

That will leave us with the following code:

```php
// Ensure this file is being included by a parent file. defined('_
JEXEC') or die( "Direct Access Is Not Allowed" );

jimport('joomla.eventplugin');

class plgContentAECSubsHider extends JPlugin {

function plgContentAECSubsHider ( &$subject )
{
parent::__construct( $subject );

}

function onPrepareContent(&$article, &$params, $limitstart) {

// TODO- Adjust our regex to look for a shorter tag
//        and one collector function between the tags
$regex = "#{njaccess(.*?)}(.*?){/njaccess}#s";

$article->text = preg_replace_callback($regex,array($this,"aecsubshide
r"), $article->text);
```

```
return true;

}

function aecsubshider(&$matches) {

$user          = &JFactory::getUser();

// TODO-change this to matches[1] as we only have
//        one collector now
$output= $matches[2];

// TODO- Get the visitor's id if available.
//         If a guest (id = 0) then skip this and display
//         the please subscribe message

// TODO- Look for the id in the AEC subscriptions
//         table, and check if they have a valid, paid
//         subscription. If so, return the text
//         if not, skip it and return the message

// TODO- Instead of blank, return our message from our
//       language file
return "";

}

}
```

For our `regex`, we could change it to {aecsubshider}text to hide{/
aecsubshider}, but that is even longer than it is now and not exactly easier
to type. Instead, let's shorten it further to the idea we had earlier, soc—subscriber
only content. This will leave us with {soc}text for subscribers{/soc} which
is much easier to type.

So let's change our `regex` pattern to the new tags, and only one collector.

```
$regex = "#{soc}(.*?){/soc}#s";
```

Next, let's do the quick change to our `$output` declaration so it can handle the new
single collector.

```
$output= $matches[1];
```

Next up, we need to get our visitor's user id.

Add in the following code, and change the comments:

```
$output= $matches[1];
// Get the visitor's id if available.
// If a guest (id = 0) then skip this and display
// the please subscribe message
$userid = $user->get('id');

if ( !$userid )
{
// TODO- Look for the id in the AEC subscriptions
//        table, and check if they have a valid, paid
//        subscription. If so, return the text
//        if not, skip it and return the message

}
```

Here we said `if(!$userid)`. What does this mean? An exclamation mark in PHP indicates that something **IS NOT**, `!=` for example means NOT equal to.

So we are saying `if (IS NOT $userid)`. Well it still doesn't make much sense does it? This is because in PHP a value of 0 is considered to be the same as FALSE and any value other than 0 is considered to be TRUE. So what this is in effect saying is `if($userid IS NOT 0)` then do something. A userid of 0 indicates that this is a guest.

Now we need to work out a query to find out if our user has a valid paying subscription.

First, like with our module, we will open up EasySQL and try to find the AEC tables.

And as before, they are pretty easy to spot.

Looking down that list, the one most likely to hold our subscription data is
`jos_acctexp_subscr`. Sure enough, if we do a `select *` query in EasySQL
with it, we will see that it contains exactly the sort of columns we are looking for.
Particularly:

- `userid` — the id of our user

- `status` — the status will be either Active, Expired or Excluded

- `plan` — the id of the AEC subscription plan

With these three fields we can find out which users have an active paying subscription.

Before we build our query, we need to know the ids for our paying plans. Lets use
EasySQL again and do a `select *` query on the table `jos_acctexp_plans`. The
results tell us that plan ids 1, 2, and 3 are our paying plans. If we were to add a free
plan now, it would be id 4 so not included in our query.

 If we were making this plugin to distribute, we would use a parameter for
the plan ids and ask the user to enter the plan ids. Since this is our own
site, and it won't be changing often, if at all, hard coding is fine.

So now we can build our query. It will look something like this:

```
SELECT count(*)
FROM
jos_acctexp_subscr
WHERE userid = $userid
AND ((status = "Active" AND plan IN (1,2,3))
OR (status = "Excluded"))
```

Of course, we still need to format it and put it into PHP but that is the structure it
will take.

Why are we only selecting `count(*)`? Because we don't actually need any data from
this query apart from a yes or no that this user has a valid subscription. In SQL, the
asterisk character, `*`, is used to indicate "all columns" so we are saying please count
all columns. We could just specify a single column such as `count(userid)`, which
would make the query a tiny bit faster, but we need to be careful that we don't count
a column that can contain null values, or it may change our results.

Remember above how we discussed that `0 = FALSE`, so if our count returns 0 it is
the same as returning FALSE, and if it returns 1 or more, then it is the same as
returning TRUE.

Also, why did we split up the two statuses `Active` and `Excluded`?

Excluded is a special status that is reserved for people who don't need a subscription, for example administrators. Giving an administrator a subscription might limit what they can do on the site, and we don't want to have to make a special 'unlimited powers' subscription just for administrators. So to fix this, administrators and other special people can simply be given that status of `Excluded` in order to avoid being affected by the subscription system, and in this case our content hider as well.

So now let's build it. Remember that first we need to create a database object, write our query, set the query, and finally load our records. Don't forget to fix up our comments either.

```
if ( !$userid )
{

// Look for the id in the AEC subscriptions
// table, and check if they have a valid, paid
// subscription. If so, return the text
// if not, skip it and return the message

$db = &JFactory::getDBO();

$query ='SELECT count(*)
        FROM jos_acctexp_subscr
            WHERE userid = "'.$userid.'"
            AND ((status = "Active" AND plan IN (1,2,3))
            OR (status = "Excluded")) ';

$db->setQuery($query);

$count = $db->loadResult();

}
```

Notice that we used `$db->loadResult` instead of `$db->loadObjectList`, which we used in our module. This is because here we only need the first value of the first record and not a complete list of objects with various fields, which is what `$db->loadResult` is designed to return.

So now, we have our answer to the question "is this person a paying subscriber?", but what do we do with it? We will check it to see that it is not 0, and if it isn't, we will return the text. If, however, it is 0, then we will do nothing and continue to the next return, which returns our "please subscribe" message.

Before we display our message though, we need to do a little work. By default, Joomla! doesn't load language strings for pugins on the front end. So we will have to manually load the language file for our plugin, and then we can use it.

```
if ($count)
    return $output;

$lang = & JFactory::getLanguage();
$lang->load('plg_content_aecsubshider', JPATH_ADMINISTRATOR);

return JText::_( 'Hidden' );
```

`JText::_()` is a function we can use to help us access the text inside our language files. Here we are calling the `Hidden` key from our language file, which contains our "please subscribe" message. When we enter our text into the `JText::_()` function, it can be in any case we like. What is important is that the Key in the language file itself is always in uppercase.

There is a lot more to language files than what is covered here. Please refer to the Joomla! documentation for more information.

aecsubshider.xml

Our XML manifest is the last file we need to change, and thankfully it is a fairly simple one, with no surprises. If we follow the comments we placed earlier, we will remove the unneeded files, rename the others, and change the description.

While we are here, we may as well update the author information to indicate ourselves, because we are now the new author of this extension.

This leaves us with the following file:

```
<?xml version="1.0" encoding="utf-8"?>
<install version="1.5" type="plugin" group="content">
    <name>AEC Subscription Hider</name>
<author>Daniel Chapman</author>
<creationDate>February 2009</creationDate>
<copyright>(C) 2009 Your Japanese House</copyright>
    <license>http://www.gnu.org/copyleft/gpl.html GNU/GPL</license>
    <authorEmail>daniel@yourjapanesehouse.com</authorEmail>
    <authorUrl>www.yourjapanesehouse.com</authorUrl>
    <version>1.0</version>
<description>AECSUBSHIDER DESC</description>
<files>
<filename plugin="aecsubshider">aecsubshider.php</filename>
    </files>
<params>
```

```
    </params>
    <languages>
    <language tag="en-GB">en-GB.plg_content_aecsubshider.ini</language>
        </languages>
    </install>
```

We should now be able to package up our plugin and install it.

Step 4: Install and test our Plugin

A mistake I often make myself when testing a new plugin is forgetting to enable it after I install it. So we should make sure we go to the **Plugin Manager** and enable our AEC Subscriptions Hider plugin before we start.

Now we can create a new article and put some text into it.

```
A test article
```

```
{soc}hidden text{/soc}
```

This isn't particularly complicated, but enough to test.

Now make sure we are logged out on the front end of our site, and thus a guest. Let's see what we get.

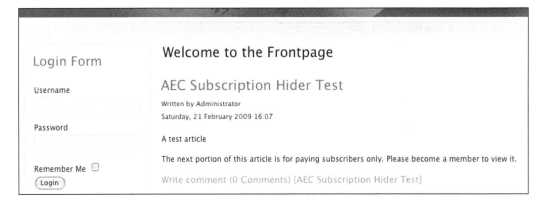

Looks great! Now let's try the reverse and login to see what we get.

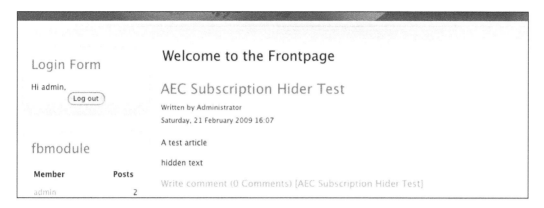

Perfect. Now we can hide our best content from non-subscribers, and hopefully entice them to subscribe.

If we wanted to, we now also have the ability to take the Ninja Access Module and make the same changes to it so we can show and hide modules depending on the visitor's subscription status.

Summary

Congratulations! We have now finished our first successful plugin customization and cleaned out a lot of unnecessary code as well. We should now have an understanding of:

- How a plugin is constructed
- The types of plugins
- plugin events
- plugin order
- The different types of files we need for a plugin
- How to customize a plugin

We should now be comfortable enough to study and make changes to any plugin we wish.

8
Customizing Components

So far we have made changes to templates, modules, and plugins. Now, it's time for components.

As we go through the customization process, it's worth remembering that our main aim is not to learn everything right here. That would make this book impossibly long and boring to read. Our aim is instead to build our confidence in examining, researching, and making changes by looking at some basic changes to existing extensions. Through this, we will build an understanding of how these extensions work and how they are assembled. This understanding will then lead to confidence because when we know the basics, we can build upon them.

For many Joomla! site owners, it is learning these basics that poses the biggest problem for them. Without the understanding and confidence to make their desired changes, they are left paralyzed, either with a site they want to complete but are unable to, or with expensive bills for contracted developers they need to hire just to perform simple tasks.

So our intention by the end of this book is to not have perfected our skills as a professional developer, but rather to have increased our confidence to the point that we are able to pick up an extension and begin making changes to it.

With that said, let's look at our components.

Components are the bread and butter of our web site. They provide all of the main functionality we require for the operation of our site.

Similar to modules, components are often visible on the front end of our site, and also usually on the administrator side as well. Unlike modules however, there is only a single component displayed on a page, but there can be many modules.

Some modules and even components can load other components inside themselves. So, if we have an unusual project that requires two components to be loaded onto the same page, it is theoretically possible, but it is not normal.

Components are arguably the most powerful extensions, allowing for a much greater range of control than modules and plugins.

Over this chapter we are going to:

- Look briefly at the makeup of components
- Discuss at some of the differences between component development methods
- Discuss the ideas of MVC development in more detail
- Make some changes to the design of one of the components on our own site in order to integrate it into our template more cleanly

Component composition and operation

With some careful coding, a simple component at its most basic could be assembled with only two files, an XML manifest and a PHP file. In practical use however, the vast majority of components will have at least three files. If they are written according to the best practices for Joomla! Extension development, they will be more likely to have at least 5-10 files. A very complex component, such as a shopping cart or forum, can easily have 50 or more files.

With so many files floating around, how do we know what is what?

This really depends on how the extension was developed. A well-written extension should be organized according to best practices, with similar files grouped together in separate folders. Then it should be relatively straightforward to understand what the files do.

Out with the old, in with the new—MVC

With the release of Joomla! 1.5, the way components were constructed and how they operated changed considerably.

The biggest change was the move to a new Model View Controller (MVC) architecture, which we looked at very briefly before.

Before MVC

Pre-MVC components generally had fewer files and folders, but those files contained a lot more programming code, and often mixed processes such as data processing, display code, and business logic in the same files.

This made the files larger, less flexible, more error prone, and more difficult to work with.

 For compatibility purposes, components can still be run under Joomla! 1.5 using this older architecture, but it is highly recommended that new extensions use the new MVC style.

If we unzipped a typical pre-MVC extension, we would see a file structure similar to the following:

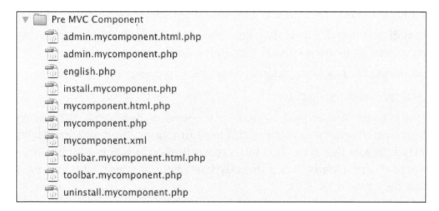

The main files in an installation like this are:

- `admin.mycomponent.html.php`

  This file contains a class with display functions for all of the admin side screens contained in it. The functions are usually called directly from `admin.mycomponent.php` and passed any data they need to display.

- `admin.mycomponent.php`

  This contains all of the primary action and data manipulation functions for the admin side, all wrapped in a class. Sometimes, in a large extension, this may simply contain calls to other files that do the actual processing separately.

- `install.mycomponent.php`

   This file is executed after the extension is installed. It typically contains functions that do things like insert default data into the database statements, set file permissions, or do updates that couldn't be done automatically through the Joomla! installer.

   If an extension requires no such functions, then this file will usually be omitted.

   If it is included, then it gets its own personal reference in the component's XML manifest file and is not included in the usual `<files>` tag.

   `<installfile>install.mycomponent.php</installfile>`

- `uninstall.mycomponent.php`

   This file serves the opposite function of the previous file, and is executed when a component is uninstalled. It is usually used to clean up the database or file system.

   As with the install file, it may be omitted, but if included, needs to be referenced in its own special way in the XML manifest file.

   `<uninstallfile>uninstall.mycomponent.php</uninstallfile>`

- `mycomponent.html.php`

   Similar to its counterpart, `admin.mycomponent.html.php`, this file contains a class with display functions in it. These functions, however, are for the front end of the site this time. It is the screens that our visitors will be seeing. The functions are usually called directly from `mycomponent.php` and passed any data they need to display.

- `mycomponent.php`

   This contains all of the primary action and data manipulation functions for the front end of our site, all wrapped in a class. Like `admin.mycomponent.php`, this may sometimes contain calls to other files that do the actual processing separately.

- `mycomponent.xml`

   This is our XML manifest file. Components, like every other extension, must always contain one of these if they want to use the Joomla! installer.

- `toolbar.mycomponent.php`

   This contains logic for the admin side toolbar.

- `toolbar.mycomponent.html.php`

  This contains the HTML for the admin side toolbar.

- `english.php`

  Older language files didn't have the language-region name conventions, and instead were just a simple language name, such as `english.php`, `spanish.php`, and so on. This system was a little inflexible as it didn't take into account that there are variants and dialects for almost all of the major languages, for example, does `english.php` contain British or American English?

After MVC

MVC components, on the other hand, usually have significantly more individual files and folders than their predecessors, but each file contains a lot less programming code. True MVC components are also much more segregated, with clear separation between business logic, data management, and displayed views.

This results in a file structure that looks more confusing initially, but is actually much, much easier to work with. It is also more powerful, for several reasons.

First, finding the code we want to change is much faster and easier because of the segregation. If we want to edit a display screen, we go to the `views` directory, or the way data is loaded we go to the `models` directory, or the way a save is processed we look in the `controllers` folder, and so on.

Second, making changes to one aspect of the component without impacting others is easier. For example, a view can be edited to change the way it displays data without necessarily having to edit any of the code that handles loading that data. This keeps components much more stable.

Then there is the ease of replacing different views with another one. With the MVC setup, a template can make use of template overrides, and load their own modified copy of an extension's view instead of the original developer's view and thus style it to suit their template. This is impossible with the pre-MVC system.

There are more advantages, but these are the key ones.

Now, if we unzipped a typical MVC extension we would see a file structure similar to this:

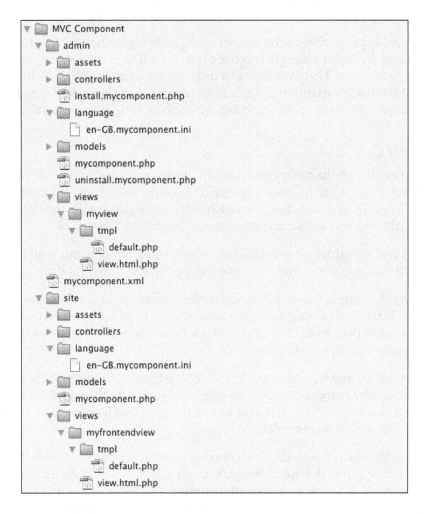

The first thing we will notice is that the main files in our installation are broken up into two subfolders, admin and site. This is not actually a forced requirement, and if we really wanted to, we could still name our files mycomponent.php and admin.mycomponent.php and so on. However, the best practice is to divide them like this for easier management. With an MVC component, it is often easier to talk about directories and their purpose, rather than just files and their purpose as we do with pre-MVC components. The relevant files and folders for an MVC component are:

- admin/mycomponent.php

  This is our initial admin file. It will check the parameters that were passed in through the URL, and for a simple component it may do the processing itself. In an advanced component, it will then load and execute the controller and task corresponding to the URL request.

- admin/assets/

  The assets folder is usually used to contain CSS, JavaScript, and image files, as well as any other media files or program helper files.

  Some developers prefer to create separate directories admin/javascript, admin/css, and so on. It is, however, preferred to bundle them into the assets folder.

- admin/controllers/

  In the controllers folder, we will have all of our controller definition files. These contain the bulk of our business logic with each file containing a controller class. Basic controllers will usually contain the functions listed (below) inside them, and each function corresponds to a task that the controller performs. If we use the names below for our functions, then we can make use of the default Joomla! toolbar buttons as they call these functions:

  - display—calls the default view for the controller
  - save—used to save a record to the database and return to a main screen
  - edit—used to save a record to the database and return to the same screen
  - remove—used to delete a record from the database
  - publish—publishes an item

  In complex components there will also often be other functions.

- admin/language/

  The admin/language/ folder is used to hold language files for our administrator interface. While, far away, the most common language file prefix is en-GB, many extensions do come with several languages included by default, so this folder may contain more files.

> When we install a component, language files are not copied to the components directory like most files are. Instead, they are copied to the language/ folder on the Joomla! root. This is so that all Joomla! language files are organized in the same place.

- `admin/models/`

  The `admin/models/` folder contains the data models we use for retrieving data needed by our controllers and views. Models are used most often for listing rows based on criteria, performing searches, manipulating data, and handling pagination.

- `admin/tables/`

  The `admin/tables/` folder holds class definitions that correspond to all of the tables used by our application. Table classes differ from models in that they are usually accessed using the `id` column of the table, and are usually used to retrieve specific records for editing, saving, and deleting. If model classes were data shotguns, table classes would be sniper rifles.

- `admin/views/`

  The `admin/views/` folder is more complex than the other folders above and contains a series of subfolders. There will be one folder for each administrator view in our extension.

- `admin/views/myview/view.html.php`

  In the first directory for each of our views, we will almost always have a file called `view.html.php`. This is our view file itself and arranges the data we have retrieved, usually from a model or table, into something meaningful and ready to be displayed.

  Like many things in a Joomla! component, this file has a naming convention. This convention follows `view.output_type.php`. While HTML is our most common output type, we can also have views for RSS feeds, PDF documents, raw or error outputs for the same view.

  We will only be concerning ourselves with the HTML option, however, at this time.

- `admin/views/myview/tmpl/default.php`

  In the `tmpl` sub directory of our views, there will be a file called `default.php`. This is a layout file and contains the HTML that the view needs in order to display itself. It is passed the assembled data by the view file, and then lays it out to be displayed.

  There will also often be other files in this directory, each one indicating a different layout, that might be set by preferences or depending on the data. Some of them may be sub-templates, containing portions of HTML that are then loaded into the main layout file.

- `admin/install.mycomponent.php`

  Just like with our pre-MVC component, this file is executed after the extension is installed, and typically contains functions that do things like insert default data into the database statements, set file permissions, or do updates that couldn't be done automatically through the Joomla! installer.

  If an extension requires no such functions, then this file will usually be omitted.

  If it is included, then it gets its own personal reference in the component's XML manifest file and is not included in the usual `<files>` tag.

  `<installfile>install.mycomponent.php</installfile>`

- `admin/uninstall.mycomponent.php`

  This file serves the opposite function of the previous file and is executed when a component is uninstalled. It is usually used to clean up the database or file system.

  As with the install file, it may be omitted, but if included it needs to be referenced in its own special way in the XML manifest file.

  `<uninstallfile>uninstall.mycomponent.php</uninstallfile>`

- `site/mycomponent.php`

  This contains all of the primary action and data manipulation functions for the front end of our site, all wrapped in a class. Like `admin/mycomponent.php`, this may do the processing itself. In an advanced component, it will then load and execute the controller and task corresponding to the URL request.

- `site/assets/`
- `site/controllers/`
- `site/language/`
- `site/models/`
- `site/tables/`
- `site/views/`

  These folders all contain files that perform essentially the exact same activities as the corresponding admin folders.

- `mycomponent.xml`

  This is our XML manifest file. MVC components, like every other extension, must always contain one of these if they want to use the Joomla! installer.

Execution flow for components

MVC and Pre-MVC components execute in roughly the same manner, but MVC components have a couple of extra steps as a result of the file segregation. Some of these steps are in fact useful, allowing for things like overrides of the layout.

The execution flow is best illustrated in the following figures.

Firstly is the Pre-MVC execution method:

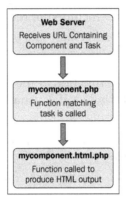

Next is the MVC execution method:

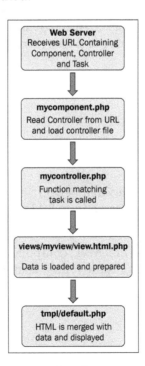

Customizing components

Components are considerably more difficult to make changes to than any other extension, and so we must take great care when working with them.

Usually, most web site developers will be happy with the functionality provided, but sometimes we can make slight tweaks to a component in order to give our web site a little bit of extra functionality.

However, there is one kind of common change many web site owners will, and should, make to their components. That change is to customize the appearance of the components so that they blend with the template.

If we remember our earlier discussion on the Frankensite syndrome, unmatched templates and components are one of the most common examples of this. It makes it immediately obvious that our site is either a CMS, a mash-up of different scripts, or just run by someone with terrible taste. We don't want people thinking any of these about our web business.

Because we want our business to succeed, we need to make some changes to the installed components, so that they better match our template.

This should give us some starting experience with modifying components and the confidence to customize the rest of our site as needed.

Also, understanding and working with the code of a component is usually much more difficult than a module or plugin. It is especially difficult when a component performs multiple, or complex functions, as many do. Conversely, a module or plugin usually only performs one or two simple functions.

Because of this difficulty, many developers, when customizing a component, only focus on the sections of the component they need to learn in order to make their changes. We will follow the same example and will only look at the sections we need to know.

We will also compress our process from the previous two chapters, combining understanding the code and planning, marking and making our changes into a single step for each thing we want to change. The reason for this is that we aren't undertaking major development and merely tweaking the output, so there isn't a need for the extended process.

The third important change from the previous two chapters is that with modules and plugins, we worked with them before installation, packaged them up, and finally installed them. With components, however, we have already installed them, so we will edit a copy of the appropriate files on our PC and upload only the files we edit.

Customizing component output

The customization we will look at is our component output. Specifically, we want to make our forum look more integrated into our site. If we look at our forum, it doesn't quite match our template. The black headings are too dark, and even though the boxes have round corners like the rest of our site, they are a little too sharp when compared to our modules.

When making customizations of this nature, the best thing to do is to reuse the CSS and images from the template as much as possible. This way, we are almost guaranteed to get a smooth integration.

Keeping that in mind, we can look over our template and find some graphics that suit our forum's basic structure.

As the forum front page is divided into boxes, with a size and shape similar to a module, taking some of the module styling seems like a good idea. This can especially be applied to the body of the forum boxes.

The header area though, which is currently black, may not look as good if we used the module styling, and may give the forum a washed out look, possibly making the boxes look a little too much like modules. We could, however, take the background coloring from the very top menu, which is the darkest part of our template, and use that instead of the black.

This dark blue from the top menu would also be appropriate for our buttons, so we will use it for them as well.

Change 1: Adding rounded corners to the forum

When working with a component's front end design, it is often more useful to look at the design live, and examine the HTML as it appears rather than reading lines of code and trying to imagine how they will be output.

Luckily, we have Firebug and we can use the **Inspect Element** tool to have the best of both worlds, seeing it live and being able to drill into the HTML structure at the same time.

Let's start with putting some round corners on the bottom of our gallery.

In modern web development, round corners are commonly created via nesting four HTML elements, usually `div` elements, inside one another. Then four carefully designed background images are placed in each of those HTML elements and carefully positioned to overlap each other, giving the appearance of rounded corners while still remaining flexible enough to be variable width and height.

We only want to put rounded corners on the bottom two corners, so we will only need two HTML elements nested inside each other. Looking at our existing forum design, it already has rounded corners on the bottom, so it is very likely that we will have at least two nested HTML elements.

The quickest way to find out is to right-click on one of our bottom corners and then select **Inspect Element** from the menu. We should see something like this:

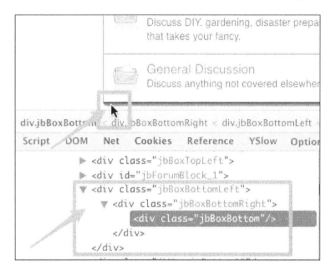

By the looks of it, our forum's design may not quite be what we are looking for. Instead of being four `div`s nested inside each other, the bottom corners of our forum are completely separate from the main body and consists of three `div`s nested inside each other; one small `div` for each corner and one long for the bottom.

This poses a slight problem for us as we not only want to transfer the corners over from the module, but also the light gradient at the bottom. If we were to put enough padding in this bottom area to show the gradient properly, we would end up with a huge empty space at the bottom of every section of our forum.

Ok then, what about the body of each section? Are there any nested `div`s in there we can use?

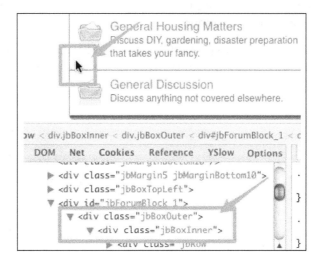

We see that each of our forum section's main body has two nested `div`s with the classes `jbBoxOuter` and `jbBoxInner`. This is exactly what we need. We can put the rounded corners and the gradient onto these `div`s, and hide the three nested bottom `div`s.

Before we assign our new corners, we first need to find out where the images for the round corners are. The easiest way to do this is via an inspect element on a module.

If we do this, and then expand the HTML for the module, we can see that there are four nested `div`s. If we examine each `div` in turn we should see something like this:

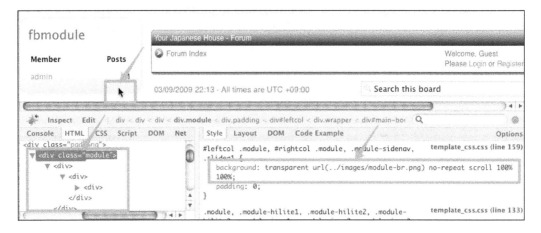

We only need the images from the outermost two `divs`, the bottom-left and -right images, and we want to put them into our forum. The easiest way to do this is to cut and paste the image CSS from the template into the forum component, then adjust it to point to the images correctly.

Before we do that, we should prepare our environment so it is ready to go when we want to start changing the code.

Because we are changing the component's design, we will mainly be working with CSS. We will need to open up the CSS file that we want to make changes to.

First, unzip a copy of the forum into a development area on your local PC. As I mentioned above, we won't be repacking the component and installing it, rather we will just be uploading the changed files one by one into an already installed component.

Now that we have our component unzipped, we could go looking through all the files trying to find our CSS file, or we can take a shortcut.

The shortcut is to use Firebug again. If we remember, in the top-right-hand corner of the tabs that appear, when we click **Inspect Element**, there is a link to the file that the CSS comes from and the line which it comes from as well. In this case, our file is called `joobb_black.css`. We can see this here:

If we right-click on this link and select **Open in New Tab**, we can see our CSS file has been loaded up for us.

Now this by itself isn't very useful as we can't edit this file, only view it. What is important, however, is the address bar at the top of the page. It tells us exactly where our file is located, as shown here:

Now that we know our file is located on the server in the directory:

```
components/com_joobb/designs/styles/joobb_black/joobb_black.css
```

We can trim this down further by ignoring the `components/com_joobb` directory, and the remainder will show us where to look in our unzipped component.

```
designs/styles/joobb_black/joobb_black.css
```

We can now go straight to the location of the CSS file for our forum and open it up in our favorite code IDE.

Now that we have the CSS file open, we will go back to our front end and work out what changes to make.

Before putting the images into the footer of our forum, we first need to find out where they are as well. Let's inspect a module again and find the location of the background images.

If we look at the background CSS attribute for the `divs` around our module, we will find the following:

```
transparent url(../images/module-br.png) no-repeat scroll 100% 100%
```

The most important part here is `../images/module-br.png` which tells us that from the location of our CSS file, the images are one level up, indicated by the dot, dot, slash: `../`. Then we go down one level into the images directory.

Image references in CSS can either be an absolute reference from the web site location, for example, `http://mysite.com/images/image.png`, or they can be relative to the location of the CSS file itself, for example, `/images/image.png`.

We can use whichever one is most appropriate to our situation. In most cases, we will use relative notation, but absolute can be used if the image is on a different domain, or in a directory very distant to the one the CSS file is in.

So, where is our CSS file then? We can find this one the same way we found the CSS file for our forum. Open it up in a new tab and check the address bar.

Doing so reveals this to us:

```
http://yourjapanesehouse.com/templates/rt_vertigo_j15/css/template_
css.css
```

From here, we can see our CSS file is in our template's `css` directory. If we go one level up, and then down into the images folder, our images should be located in the folder:

```
http://yourjapanesehouse.com/templates/rt_vertigo_j15/images/
```

If we now check the image names again, we want to move across the images `module-br.png` and `module-bl.png` to our forum. Because our forum CSS file is located in the components directory, and the images are located in the templates directory, a relative reference in our CSS would look like this:

```
../../../../../templates/rt_vertigo_j15/images/module-br.png
```

and an absolute reference would look like this:

```
http://yourjapanesehouse.com/templates/rt_vertigo_j15/images/ module-
br.png
```

It is up to us to decide which one we would like to use. The absolute reference is easier to understand, but the relative reference is a little bit shorter.

Now that we know how to reach our image from our forum's CSS file, we need to work out where to put these references.

Let's inspect the body of a forum section and find out where they are controlled in our forum CSS file. Let's use their classes as a name, so they are easier to speak about. `jbBoxOuter`, has its CSS starting at line 37 and `jbBoxInner` starts at line 41.

If we look in our `joobb_black.css` at line 37 and below, we will see the following CSS for these two `div`s:

```
.jbBoxOuter {
    width: 100%;
}
.jbBoxInner {
    height: 100%; /* IE */
    border-left: 1px solid #999793;
    border-right: 1px solid #999793;
}
```

The first change we will make is to remove the two border attributes from `jbBoxInner`, leaving us with only:

```
.jbBoxInner {
    height: 100%; /* IE */
}
```

Next, we want to add our new background images. If we use the original module as a guide, `module-br.png` should be on the outermost `div`.

```
.jbBoxOuter {
    width: 100%;
    background:
    url(../../../../../templates/rt_vertigo_j15/images/module-br.png)
    100% 100% no-repeat;
}
.jbBoxInner {
height: 100%; /* IE */
    background:
    url(../../../../../templates/rt_vertigo_j15/images/module-bl.png)
    0 100% no-repeat;
}
```

Now, let's save and upload this file to our site and see what happens to our forum.

To upload our file we could use either FTP or NinjaXplorer. For single files like this, I usually prefer NinjaXplorer, so we will use that.

On our site admin, go to **Components | NinjaXplorer** and then navigate to the directory were our Forum CSS is, `components/com_joobb/designs/styles/joobb_black/`. Then use the upload button in the icon menu at the top and select our `joobb_black.css` file.

Now we can go back to our front-end view of the forum and refresh our page. We should see something like this:

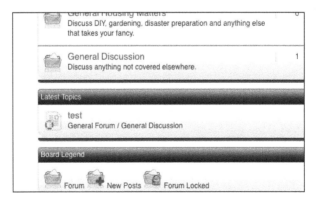

Well our corners are in place, and so is the gradient. However, there are some extra images there that we don't need, mainly the black bottom area.

To get rid of this bottom area, we have three choices:

- Edit the HTML for the forum and delete them, then remove any references to them from the CSS

- Add a `display:none` attribute to the CSS of the outermost `div`, making them all disappear

- Remove all CSS references to them, leaving them on the page, but effectively invisible because they have no styling

If we wanted to be completely professional about this, we should take option 1. However, there are some drawbacks to us taking this route. We would need to edit potentially complicated files and risk breaking our forum. It will also take longer to make and test the changes. Possibly the most important is that if we want to update our forum in the future to a new version, then we will have to recheck the updated code, redo the changes, and retest it. If we just use CSS to hide it, then all we need to do for an update is take a copy of our CSS file, update the forum, and then copy our old CSS file over the new on.

So while options 2 and 3 are not best practice for an experienced professional programmer, they do provide us with the quickest, easiest, and safest route for making these changes as an intermediate level developer working on our own site.

As a result, we will choose option 3 because it is just as easy to implement as option 2, but makes our CSS files a tiny bit smaller, improving page load times by a fraction of a second. Also, not rendering any CSS is quicker than rendering a `display:none`, so we get another performance increase there, however small.

Option 2 would be best for us if it were a temporary change, such as for testing. But we won't use this CSS again so removing it completely is best.

Looking in Firebug, we can see that the CSS for these three `divs` is in `joobb_black.css` and the three `divs` start on lines 47, 53, and 59 respectively.

Let's go into `joobb_black.css` and remove all the CSS for those three classes.

If we upload our CSS file and refresh our page again, we should now see something similar to this:

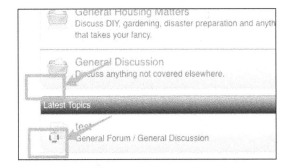

We are very close to finishing this, but we are not quite there yet. The last thing we have to fix is the gray line that we can see below our curved corners. If we look around with Firebug at the different divs inside jbBoxInner, then we will quickly spot a class called jbBorderBottom. If we take a look at the CSS for the class it only has:

```
.jbBorderBottom {
border-bottom:1px solid #DBDBDB;
}
```

Similar to our black bottom section, we don't need this CSS at all, and won't in the future, so we can just delete it. According to Firebug it is on line 239.

Now we should see our corners looking like the ones here:

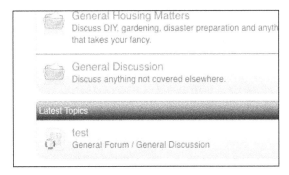

Change 2: Replace the heading background

Now that we have our nice rounded corners on the bottom, it's time to make the heading area at the top of our forum sections fit our site template more closely.

Adding the same rounded corners will make our forum look too washed out, as the module corners are quite pale and subtle. We want something a bit bolder instead.

Looking around our template, we have our grassy green footer and our blue top menu bar.

We don't really want people to mentally associate our forum headers with the page footer, so using the top menu bar is our best bet. Also useful is the fact that the text on the top menu bar and the forum header bars is all white, so we don't need to change the text, only the background.

Using what we learned when adding rounded corners to our forum sections, changing the header background will be quite straightforward.

The first thing we need to do is identify where the image is. Let's inspect the top menu bar and find its background CSS attribute. If we scroll down slightly in Firebug we will find the following:

```
#horiz-menu {                                style1.css (line 42)
background:transparent url(../images/style1/horiz-menu-bg.png) repeat-
x scroll 0 0;
}
```

From this, we can click on the value for the background CSS property and copy it to our clipboard.

Next, let's inspect one of our forum headers and see how they are organized.

As shown in the following screenshot, we can see that the header background is comprised of 3 `div`s, one for each corner and one for the middle of the page with classes of `jbBoxTopLeft`, `jbBoxTopRight`, and `jbBoxTop` respectively.

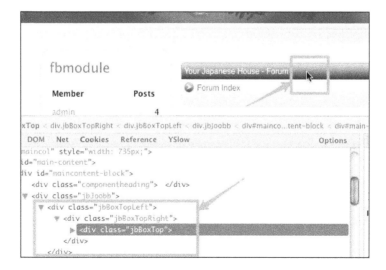

Currently, each of these has a different image set for their background giving it the rounded corners look. We won't be worrying about the rounded corners, and we just want to display the same background as the top header.

As we only want to display one background image, we can just remove the background images from the two inner most `div`s, `jbBoxTopRight` and `jbBoxTop`. We should put the background image on the outermost `div` because it will almost always be the largest.

Looking in Firebug, we can see that the CSS for these three starts on lines 19, 25, and 31. Looking at our CSS file, we find:

```
.jbBoxTop {
    background: url(images/boxTop.png) repeat-x;
    width: 100%;
    height: 25px;
}

.jbBoxTopLeft {
    background: url(images/boxTopLeft.png) 0 0 no-repeat;
    height: 25px;
    padding-left: 5px;
}

.jbBoxTopRight {
    background: url(images/boxTopRight.png) 100% 0 no-repeat;
    height: 25px;
    padding-right: 5px;
}
```

The first thing we want to do now is take the background CSS property we copied from the top menu bar and paste it into `jbBoxTopLeft`, which is our outermost `div`.

```
.jbBoxTopLeft {
    background: transparent url(../images/style1/horiz-menu-bg.png)
    repeat-x scroll 0 0;
    height: 25px;
    padding-left: 5px;
}
```

Now this isn't going to work yet, because we need to put in the path to the template directory like we did for our rounded corners.

```
.jbBoxTopLeft {
    background: transparent
    url(../../../../../templates/rt_vertigo_j15/images/style1/
    horiz-menu-bg.png) repeat-x scroll 0 0;
    height: 25px;
    padding-left: 5px;
}
```

Now let's remove the background from the other two `divs` and we will be left with the CSS below. In fact, we don't need any styling at all on the other `divs` so we can just remove it all leaving us only with `jbBoxTopLeft`.

```
.jbBoxTopLeft {
    background: transparent
    url(../../../../../templates/rt_vertigo_j15/images/style1/
    horiz-menu-bg.png) repeat-x scroll 0 0;
    height: 25px;
    padding-left: 5px;
}
```

If we save and upload this file, then go back to our forum and refresh the page, we should now have a nice blue bar for our forum header like in this:

Something isn't quite right here. Our forum headers are a lot shorter than the top bar. This isn't a problem, but it does look a little odd. If we inspect our top menu bar, and move our mouse over the background property, a small tool tip will pop up telling us the size of our top bar image.

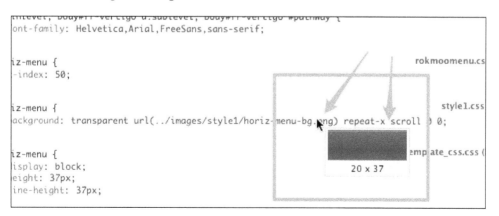

From here, we can see that our image is 37 pixels tall. Looking back at our CSS, we can see that our forum header is set to be 25 pixels tall. If we want to see the whole image, we need to increase the height of our header bar.

```
.jbBoxTopLeft {
   background: transparent
   url(../../../../../templates/rt_vertigo_j15/images/style1/
   horiz-menu-bg.png) repeat-x scroll 0 0;
   height: 37px;
   padding-left: 5px;
}
```

Once saved and uploaded, we can refresh the page and our header is certainly bigger, and looks more matched with the top. Now, the text is off center. We really want to move it down a few pixels.

Moving text inside a `div` can be done in two ways. First, we can use padding or margins to move it manually. Alternatively, we can give it a `line-height` CSS attribute and let the browser position it automatically, central to the `line-height` which we set.

If we inspect our forum header text, we find it is attached to a class `jbTextHeader`. This class has its CSS on line 67.

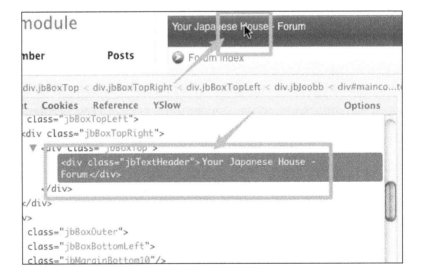

We can see in Firebug, and in the CSS file, that it already has a 5 pixel margin at the top of the text. However, we want to use the second method and attach a line height to the text, so let's remove this margin and add `line-height: 37px` to our `jbTextHeader` CSS.

```
.jbTextHeader {
color:#FFFFFF;
float:left;
    line-height:37px;
}
```

Our text should now be nicely positioned in the middle of the header, as we will see if we upload our CSS file and refresh the page.

Change 3: Replacing the buttons

The forum is looking much more integrated now. The only thing left to change our buttons. This is going to be a simpler, but more time consuming, activity because we need to create new images for the buttons.

Because we used blue from the top menu bar for the headers, it might also make sense to use the same graphics on our buttons as are used around the actual menu items to keep them consistent.

Before we get into editing the button images, we need to find some images to use for our buttons.

When a template is prepared and sold by a template club, they usually prepare all the images needed for the template in one large image, so they can check for consistency and that things line up correctly. Once this large image is complete, it is "sliced" up. Slicing is the process of cutting the smaller images needed by the template's HTML out from the larger image.

This larger image is usually an Adobe Fireworks PNG file, or an Adobe Photoshop PSD file. The reason why it is usually one of these two is because these two file formats support image layers, allowing many smaller images that make up our template to be laid on top of each other. While they appear to be one image, they remain in their own layers so that they can be manipulated individually.

Once they produce the templates, good template clubs will also make the sliced images available to their customer. This is mainly so that the customers have source images to modify if they wish to change color schemes or image designs; however, we are going to use the sliced images to help us make our buttons.

If a template company provides sliced images, then they will usually be available for download in the same place as the template itself.

We already have a copy of the template source images for our template, so we will find, and take out, the source images used for the menu item backgrounds in the top menu bar and then use them to make our new buttons.

If we inspect one of the buttons, we can see that their images are stored in the directory /components/com_joobb/designs/buttons/joobb_black/en-GB/.

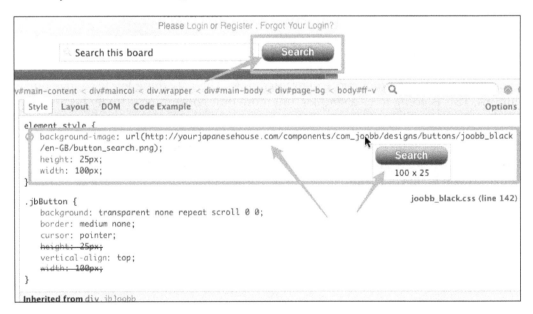

If we look in our copy of the component that we unzipped on our local machine, we will see all the buttons are there. Now we can start up our favorite image editor and replace the buttons with designs that match our template, and then upload them to the same place as the originals on our server.

There are other images and icons that we will want to change on our forum before it is 100% integrated, but those can be done in the same way as we did the buttons.

Summary

Phew! It was a long chapter, and a lot of work, but our forum is now looking a lot better than when we started. It no longer looks out of place on our site. We can now take what we learned here, and customize the output of other components, and even modules or plugins, such as our comments plugin.

We should also now understand the differences between the file and folder structure, purpose and execution flow of pre-MVC and MVC components.

This will give us the confidence we need to dive into and understand other components on our site.

9
Finding and Fixing Problems

Up to this point we have become familiar with the tools and methods for adding extensions to our site and customizing them to meet our needs. Everything has gone well for us up until this point, but as anyone who has built a complex site knows that, there will almost always be a few things that go wrong. The more complex we make our site, the more likely it is that some sort of problem will occur.

Because of this, it is vitally important for every one of us to get at least a basic understanding of how to diagnose, and preferably solve, any problems or bugs that we come across when building our site. Before we look at how to do that, we will cover some of the most common problems we may encounter when building our sites, and why they occur. We will be covering:

- Understanding common errors
- Common PHP related errors
- Common JavaScript related errors
- Common Server related errors
- Hacking the Joomla! core—consequences and considerations
- Getting Support—how to and etiquette

Understanding common errors

There are five main areas that cause the majority of problems for Joomla! sites. Understanding these areas and the common problems that occur with in each of them is a very important part of fixing them and thus, our site.

Even though there is a practically unlimited number of potential issues and problems that can occur, there are certain problems which occur much more regularly than others.

If we understand these main problems, we should be able to take care of many of the problems that will occur on our site without needing to resort to hiring people to fix them, or waiting for extension developers to provide support.

The five areas are:

- PHP code
- JavaScript code
- CSS/HTML code
- Web server
- Database

We will now look at the two most common error sources, PHP and JavaScript.

PHP code

Because PHP code is executed on the server, we usually have some control over the conditions that it is subject to.

Most PHP errors originate from one of four sources:

- Incorrect extension parameters
- PHP code error
- PHP version
- Server settings

Incorrect extension parameters

It is often easy to misunderstand what the correct value for an extension parameter is, or if a particular parameter is required or not. These misunderstandings are behind a large number of PHP "errors" that developers experience when building a site.

Diagnosis

In a well-coded extension, putting the wrong information into a parameter shouldn't result in an error, but will usually result in the extension producing strange or unexpected output, or even no output at all.

In a poorly coded extension, an incorrect parameter value will probably cause an error. These errors are often easy to spot, especially in modules, because our site will output everything it processed up until the point of the error, giving our page the appearance of being cut off.

Some very minor errors may even result in the whole page, except for the error causing extension, being output correctly, and error messages appearing in the page, where the extension with the error was supposed to appear.

A critical error, however, may cause the site to crash completely, and output only an error message. In extreme cases not even an error message will be output, and visitors will only see a white screen.

The messages should always appear in our PHP log though.

Fixing the problem

Incorrect extension parameters are the easiest problems to fix, and are often solved simply by going through the parameter screens for the extensions on the page with the errors, and making sure they all have correct values.

If they all look correct, then we may want to try changing some parameters to see if that fixes the issue. If this still doesn't work, then we have a genuine error.

PHP code error

Extension developers aren't perfect, and even the best ones can overlook or miss small issues in the code. This is especially true with large, complex extensions so please remember that even if an extension has PHP code error, it may not necessarily mean that the whole extension is poorly coded.

Diagnosis

Similar to incorrect extension parameters, a PHP coding error will usually result in a cut-off page, or a white screen, sometimes with an error message displayed, sometimes without.

Whether an error message is displayed or not depends partly on the configuration of your server, and partly on how severe the error was. Some servers are configured to suppress error output of certain types of errors.

Regardless of the screen output, all PHP errors should be output to the PHP log. So, if we get a white screen, or even get a normal screen but strange output, checking our PHP log can often help us to find the problem.

PHP logs can reside in different places on differently configured servers, although it will almost always be in a directory called `logs`. We may also not have direct access to the log, again depending on our server host. We should ask our web hosting company's support staff for the location of our PHP log, if we can't easily find it.

Some common error messages and causes are:

```
Parse error: parse error, unexpected T_STRING in…
```

This is usually caused by a missing semi-colon at the end of a line, or a missing double quote (") or end bracket ()) after we opened one. For quotes and semicolons, the problem is usually the line *above* the one reported in the error. For missing brackets, the error will sometimes occur at the end of the script, even though the problem code is much earlier in the script.

```
Parse error: syntax error, unexpected $end in…
```

We are most likely missing a closing brace (}) somewhere. Make sure that each open brace ({) we have has been closed with a closing brace (}).

```
Parse error: syntax error, unexpected T_STRING, expecting ',' or ';'
in…
```

There may be double quotes within double quotes. They either need to be escaped, using a forward slash before the inside quote, or changed to single quotes.

Fixing the problem

Fixing a PHP code error is possible but can be difficult depending on the extension.

Usually when there is a PHP code error, it will give a brief description of the error, and a line number. If nothing is being output at all, then we may need to turn error reporting up as described later.

We will then go to the line specified to examine it and the lines around it to try and find our problem. If we can't find an obvious error, then it might be better to take the error back to the developer and ask them for support.

PHP version

The current version of PHP is 5.x.x and version 6.x is expected soon, but because many older, but still popular, applications only run on PHP version 4.x.x. It is still very common to find many Web hosting companies still using PHP 4 on their servers. This problem is even more unfortunate due to the fact that PHP 4 isn't even supported anymore by the PHP developers.

In PHP 5, there are many new functions and features that don't exist in PHP 4. As a result, using these functions in an extension will cause it to error when run on a PHP 4 server.

Diagnosis

Diagnosing if we have the wrong PHP version is not obvious, as it will usually result in an error about an unknown function when the extension tries to call a function that doesn't exist in the version of PHP installed on our server.

Sometimes, the error will not be that the function is unknown, but that the number of parameters we are sending it is incorrect if they were changed between PHP 4 and PHP 5.

Fixing the problem

The only real way to fix the problem is to upgrade our PHP version. Some web hosts offer PHP 4 or 5 as an option and it might be as simple as checking a box or clicking a button to turn on PHP 5.

In case if our host doesn't offer PHP 5 at all, the only solution is to use a different extension or change our web host. This may actually be a good idea anyway, because if our host is still using an unsupported PHP version with no option to upgrade, then what other unsupported, out of date software is running those servers?

Server settings

One of the most common problems encountered by site owners in regards to server settings is file permissions.

Many web hosting companies run Linux, which uses a three-part permission model, on their servers. Using this model, every file can have separate permissions set for:

- The user who owns the particular file
- Other users in the same user group as the owner
- Everyone else (in a web site situation this is mainly the site visitors)

Each file also has three permissions that enable, or disable, certain actions on the file. These permissions are **read**, **write**, and **execute**.

Permissions are usually expressed in one of two ways, first as single characters in a file listing or as a three digit number.

For example, a file listing on a Linux server might look like this:

```
drwxr-x--- 2 auser agroup 4096 Dec 28 04:09 tmp
-rwxr-x--- 1 auser agroup 345 Sep 1 04:12 somefile.php
-rwxr--r-- 1 auser agroup 345 Sep 1 04:12 foo
```

The very first character to the left, a d or – in this case, indicates if this is a directory (the d) or a file (the -). The next nine characters indicate the permissions and who they apply to.

The first three belong to the file owner, next three to those in the same group as the owner, and the final three to everyone else.

The letters used are:

- r—read permission
- w—write permission
- x—execute permission

A dash (-) indicates that this permission hasn't been given to those particular people.

So in our example above, tmp.php can be read, written to, or executed by the owner (auser). It can be read or executed (but not written to) by other users in the same group (agroup) as the owner, but the file cannot be used at all by people outside the group. foo however, can be read by people in the owners group, and also read by everyone else, but it cannot be executed by them.

As mentioned above, permissions are also often expressed as a three-digit number. Each of the digits represents the sum of the numbers that represent the permissions granted.

For example: r = 4, w = 2, and x = 1.

Adding these together gives us a number from 0-7, which can indicate the permission level. So a file with a permission level of 644 would translate as:

6 = 4 + 2 = rw

4 = r

4 = r

or -rw-r--r-- in the first notation that we looked at.

Most servers are set by default to one of the following:

644 -rw-r--r--

755 -rwxr-xr-x

775 -rwxrwxr-x

All of this looks fine so far. The problems start to creep in depending on how the server runs their PHP. PHP can either be set up to run as the same user who owns all the files (usually our FTP user or hosting account owner), or it can be set up to run as a different user, but in the same group as the owner. Or it can be set up to be a completely different user and group, as illustrated here:

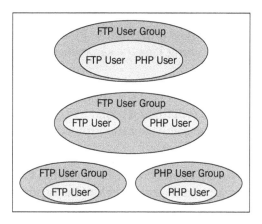

The ideal setup, from a convenience point of view, is the first one where PHP is executed as the same user who owns the files. This setup should have no problems with permissions.

But the ideal setup for a very security-conscious web host is the third one since the PHP engine can't be used to hack the web site files, or the server itself. A web server with this setup though used to have a difficult time running a Joomla! site. It was difficult because changing the server preferences requires that files be edited by the PHP user, uploading extensions means that folders and files need to be created by the PHP user, and so on.

If the PHP engine isn't even in the same group as the file owner, then it gets treated the same as any site visitor and can usually only read, and probably execute files, but not change them. This prevents us from editing preferences or uploading new extensions. However, if we changed the files so that the PHP engine could edit and execute them (permission 777, for example) then anyone who can see our site on the internet can potentially edit and execute our files by themselves, making our site very vulnerable to being hacked by even a novice hacker.

 We should never give files or directories a permission of 777 (read, write, and execute to all three user types) because it is almost guaranteed that our site will be hacked eventually as a result. If, for some reason, we need to do it for testing, or because we need to in order to install extensions, then we should change it back as soon as possible.

Diagnosis

To spot this problem is relatively simple. If we can't edit our web site configuration, or install any extensions at all, then nine times out of ten, server permissions will be the problem.

Fixing the problem

We can start by asking our web host if they allow PHP to be run as CGI, or install suEXEC (technical terms for running it as the same user who owns the files) and if so, how do we set it up.

If they don't allow this, then the next best situation is to enable the Joomla! FTP layer in our configuration. This will force Joomla! to log into our site as the FTP user, which is almost always the same user that uploaded the site files, and edit or install files.

We can enable the FTP layer by going to the **Site | Global Configuration** page and then clicking on the server item in the menu below the heading. We can then enter the required information for the FTP layer on this screen.

 The FTP layer should only be used on Linux-based servers. More information about the FTP layer can be found in the official Joomla! documentation at `http://help.joomla.org/content/view/1941/302/1/2/`

If for some reason the FTP layer doesn't work, we only have two other options. We could change our web hosting provider as one option. Or, whenever we want to install a new extension or change our configuration, we need to change the permissions on our folders, perform our tasks, and then change the permissions back to their original settings.

JavaScript code

Recently, the majority of errors on Joomla! sites seem to be related to JavaScript. This is probably because many, if not most, newer templates and extensions rely on JavaScript to operate. Because of this, many sites can have massive amounts of JavaScript being loaded on each page and if one piece of JavaScript fails, it can often bring down others. Then menus can stop working, images can stop moving, and so on.

Because JavaScript is executed on the visitor's machine and not on the web server, things that work fine in one browser on one type of operating system might not work at all on another browser or a different operating system. This can make diagnosing and fixing the errors difficult sometimes.

Joomla! site JavaScript errors are usually the result of one of three things:

- Library conflicts
- Too much JavaScript on one page
- Multiple "once per page" scripts

Library conflicts

In order to make it easier to work with JavaScript, certain groups of developers have banded together to create JavaScript libraries, which are a collection of functions that do common tasks, such as moving things around or hiding and showing them, but make them easier to use.

Many different libraries are in use around the Internet, but in the Joomla! sphere, there are two main libraries used by extension and template developers. These are Mootools and jQuery. The Mootools library is even included in Joomla!, so it's difficult to escape from this one.

 Even though Mootools and jQuery are the main libraries used, some extensions may use other libraries such as Prototype, YUI, Dojo, and so on.

When we install extensions that contain some shiny JavaScript features like sliding images or folding menus, we don't often consider the implications of that install.

For example, if your template loads a copy of Mootools, and then one of the extensions on our page also loads a copy of Mootools, then not only are we making the page unnecessarily slower, but also there is a good chance that any Mootools-related JavaScript will just fail altogether. This is especially likely on Internet Explorer, which has a fragile JavaScript engine.

The same thing can also happen if you load two different types of JavaScript library on the same page, such as a copy of Mootools and a copy of jQuery.

This is probably the most common JavaScript error I personally see, and in fact the most common error overall when working with my own Joomla! clients. Thankfully, it is usually the easiest to fix.

Diagnosis

The easiest way to spot this problem is if a page loads fine in Firefox or Safari, but all the JavaScript stops working in Internet Explorer. If this happens, then it is usually because 2 copies of the same library have been loaded.

If we have the symptoms below, then it is likely that the extensions are loading different JavaScript libraries.

- They work fine when loaded alone on a page
- One or both of them stop when loaded on he same page
- Happens in most or all browsers

If we have these symptoms, then we should right-click on our page and select the option that says **View Page Source** or something similar, as shown:.

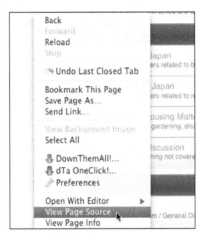

A new window or tab should now open showing us all of the HTML source code for our page, similar to the following screenshot:

```
<!DOCTYPE html PUBLIC "-//W3C//DTD XHTML 1.0 Transitional//EN" "http://www.w3.org
<html xmlns="http://www.w3.org/1999/xhtml" xml:lang="en-gb" lang="en-gb" >
        <head>
                <base href="http://yourjapanesehouse.com/" />
  <meta http-equiv="content-type" content="text/html; charset=utf-8" />
  <meta name="robots" content="index, follow" />
  <meta name="keywords" content="house japan, japanese house, buy japanese house,
  <meta name="description" content="Your Japanese House can help foreigners, gaij

  <title>Home</title>
  <link href="/feed/rss.html" rel="alternate" type="application/rss+xml" title="R
  <link href="/feed/atom.html" rel="alternate" type="application/atom+xml" title=
  <link href="/favicon.ico" rel="shortcut icon" type="image/x-icon" />
  <link rel="stylesheet" href="http://yourjapanesehouse.com/components/com_commen
  <script type="text/javascript" src="/media/system/js/mootools.js"></script>
  <script type="text/javascript" src="http://yourjapanesehouse.com/plugins/system
  <script type="text/javascript" src="http://yourjapanesehouse.com/plugins/system
  <script type="text/javascript" src="/media/system/js/caption.js"></script>
  <script type="text/javascript">

          Shadowbox.loadSkin("classic", "http://yourjapanesehouse.com/plugi
          Shadowbox.loadLanguage("en", "http://yourjapanesehouse.com/plugin
          Shadowbox.loadPlayer(["img","swf","flv","qt","wmp","iframe","html

          window.addEvent("domready", function() {

                  Shadowbox.init();
          });

</script>
```

Now, we want to check what JavaScripts are being loaded by our page. Well-written templates and extensions will usually have all their JavaScript loaded in the `<head>` section of our page. Unfortunately, however, not all extensions are well written, so we may find JavaScript being loaded anywhere on our page.

From here, we can either skim read the source looking to see which libraries are loaded, or use the browser's built-in search option to look for the word `script`. This is because every JavaScript file that is loaded will need to be within `<script>` tags.

Inside these script tags we are trying to find files with a name containing any of the following words:

- mootools
- jquery
- yui
- prototype
- scriptalicious
- dojo
- extjs

 This is not a complete list of available JavaScript frameworks, but these are some of the more popular ones available.

The filenames will sometimes have version numbers or other words in them, as seen below, but they should still be easy to recognize if we look for the aforementioned names.

Often, an extension or template will load the JavaScript library file, and then load their own files that use the library after them. The name of these supplementary files may also contain the name of the library, for example `mootools-adapter.js`, so be careful when identifying the files.

If we find multiple copies of the same library loaded, or multiple libraries loaded, then we can be confident that this is the cause of the problem.

Fixing the problem

We can fix our problem in one of two ways, depending on whether we have the same library loaded twice, or two different libraries loaded.

Same library loaded twice

If the same library is being loaded twice, we just need to stop one copy of the library being loaded. This can be done in one of three ways.

The first, and easiest, way requires that the conflicting extensions, at least one of them anyway, has been well written and has a parameter option to control whether the library is loaded or not. This option is unfortunately still not available in many extensions, but the number that supports it is growing.

The second method is very quick and dirty, and while I don't recommend it, it will fix the problem for people who don't want to change any PHP code. Simply remove, or rename, the offending library file. When the browser tries to load it, it can't find it so it will just continue on.

The third method is to edit the PHP code of our extension in question and comment out, or delete, the code that loads the JavaScript file. The script will most likely be loaded in our view files for components, and in the main file for modules and plugins. The line of code which we will want to remove will look something like:

```
$document->addScript($scriptsURL.'mootools.js');
```

When deciding which extension's library to remove, we need to make sure that we choose whichever one is loaded second. This is because there will almost always be some other JavaScript code loaded by the first extension that requires the library to be in place for it to work. If we remove the first copy of the library and not the second, then the support code from the first extension will fail, but the code from the second one will likely execute correctly.

```
r Japanese House can help foreigners, gaijin, to buy or rent thei

rnate" type="application/rss+xml" title="RSS 2.0" />
arnate" type="application/atom+xml" title="Atom 1.0" />
ut icon" type="image/x-icon" />
ourjapanesehouse.com/components/com_comment/joscomment/templates/
media/system/js/mootools.js"></script>
plugins/system/ninja_shadowbox/js/mootools.1.11.js"></script>
ttp://yourjapanesehouse.com/plugins/system/ninja_shadowbox/js/sha
media/system/js/caption.js"></script>


ssic", "http://yourjapanesehouse.com/plugins/system/ninja_shadowb
"en", "http://yourjapanesehouse.com/plugins/system/ninja_shadowbo
img","swf","flv","qt","wmp","iframe","html"], "http://yourjapanes
```

Different libraries loaded

Dealing with different libraries is a little more difficult than multiple copies of the same library. Sometimes, unfortunately, the only solution is to choose one of the extensions to remove or replace because most JavaScript libraries simply won't work with each other.

One exception to this is jQuery, which can be put into compatibility mode. This usually requires only a small amount of JavaScript code to be added, and then jQuery will be able to work with most other libraries. More information can be found at:

```
http://docs.jquery.com/Using_jQuery_with_Other_Libraries
```

If we are lucky, the extension and template developers using jQuery will have already put jQuery into compatibility mode for us, but this is not always the case.

For other libraries, there is a trick we can try that sometimes works. The trick is to try mixing up the order that the scripts are executed in, usually achieved by changing the order in which the extensions appear. More often than not this won't work, but with some simple scripts it can sometimes work.

Why this sometimes works is that after the first library is loaded, the supplementary scripts will usually be loaded. If the actions these scripts perform are done at load time, and are not repetitive, for example changing the color or loading RSS feed, then all of the scripts related to the first library finish executing before the second one is loaded. The problems creep in when the supplementary scripts of the first library are set to execute repeatedly or after the second library has loaded, for example, on click events for links or buttons or a slideshow. In this case, the supplementary scripts associated with the first library, and possibly those of the second library as well, will fail.

This trick is also more reliable in web browsers like Firefox, Safari, and Opera that have solid JavaScript engines. It most likely won't work in Internet Explorer, which, as mentioned above, has a fragile JavaScript engine.

If none of the above work, then the only thing we can do is remove, or replace, one of the extensions.

Too much JavaScript

This problem isn't very common, but if it occurs, it will usually be on Internet Explorer, especially IE6 and IE7, though it does occasionally strike other or all browsers.

If we put too many sliding panels, slideshows, shoutboxes, draggable areas, Ajax rotators, and so on into our site, the JavaScript engine will begin to get congested and slow down, get choppy and jumpy, and in some cases may even stop altogether.

This particular problem is difficult to diagnose as it may not affect people with more powerful computers, or more up to date browsers, as much it will affect people with less powerful computers or older browsers.

Diagnosis

The best way to diagnose this situation is through common sense. Have you added more than 5-10 different extensions to the same page all with JavaScript powered moving parts? Does the page load correctly when any one of the extensions is missing, but not when every one of them is loaded (meaning it isn't a conflict between any two specific extensions)?

If we answered *yes* to those two questions, then there is a good chance that we have too much JavaScript being loaded, especially if the problem only occurs in Internet Explorer.

Fixing the problem

Unless we are a professional JavaScript developer and know how we can trim the different scripts down, the only solution here really is to reduce the amount of JavaScript we are loading by removing or replacing some of our extensions.

While for some of us this may not sound like a good solution. If we have gotten our site to the point where we have so much JavaScript being loaded that it's slowing down or stopping the site, then we are very likely to have assembled a Frankensite anyway. Our site is likely to have so many moving parts that we probably give our visitors motion sickness. Keeping our site simple is almost always the best option.

Multiple "once per page" scripts

Some JavaScript is designed to run only one time per page. For example, a menu with sliding panels or an Ajax RSS feed module. This code will often have been written to look for a specific CSS `id` in an HTML tag, such as the tag below.

```
<div id="slidingmenu">…menu HTML here…</div>
```

A CSS `id` should only appear once per page, but if we were to put our sliding menu module on the same page twice, we would end up with the following:

```
<div id="slidingmenu">…menu HTML here…</div>
…some other HTML…
<div id="slidingmenu">…HTML for second menu here…</div>
```

Then when the JavaScript that activates the sliding portions of the menu is executed the first time, because it is looking for an `id`, it only executes once, on the first instance of the id, which is fine. It is when the JavaScript from the second copy of our menu is executed it again finds the first instance of the `id`, which happens to be the same as the instance the first script found.

The result being that the first copy of the menu has the JavaScript executed on itself twice, and the second copy has nothing executed on it.

Diagnosis

The easiest way to recognize this situation is when one copy of an extension works fine, but if it appears twice on a page, then only the first one, or neither of them, works.

If this occurs, check the source code of our page to see if the two extensions output identical `id`s on any of their parts.

Fixing the problem

This is a difficult issue to fix without diving into the code ourselves, so the easiest method is to take it to the developer of the extension and ask them politely to make a change to the code. They will need to put some sort of identifier into the code to make each instance of the extension unique. Using the module id or plugin id is usually the best option for this if the cause is a module or plugin.

If we can tell the developer clearly what the problem is and why, then there is a greater chance of them doing it for us.

Hacking the core

Even though the practice is dying out, there are still several extensions around that make changes to the core Joomla! files. This practice was much more common in Joomla! 1.0 than in 1.5, as 1.5 provides the ability to replace or override a lot of core functionally without having to make changes to the core code.

Most often, core hacks are used to provide enhancements or extra functionality to the user or access level systems within Joomla!, as these functions were very difficult to influence from outside the core until recently.

More commonly though, people are not hacking the core code, but making changes to the default templates included in Joomla!. Rather than acquiring a new template, they just make changes to one of the existing default ones.

Both of these practices, hacking the core and changing default templates can set site owners up for many difficulties. The most important one being that if we update our site to a newer version of Joomla!, then there is a good chance that we will replace any hacked or edited files with the ones that haven't been hacked. This means that all our work will be undone.

Many components that hack the core have a process for updating, usually involving updating to the latest version of their software, then un-hacking our site, updating Joomla!, and reapplying their hacks.

This also needs to be remembered for any extensions that we make custom changes to. When we update them, there is a good chance that it will undo any changes we made, such as to the design of our forum in the previous chapter.

In this case, we should put a copy of our edited files aside, and then once we have updated the extension, we should make the changes to the files again, using the old files as a reference. It is best not to simply copy the old file up to our server there might have been changes to the file in the update, which we would undo if we just copied the old file up.

Solving the unsolvable

There will be times where no matter what we do, we can't solve an issue with an extension ourselves. In these cases, we will have to go elsewhere for support.

Self support

Most people's first impulse is to run to the developer and ask them a question, usually on their support forum. But often there are more efficient ways to solve our problem than just dumping it on someone else. We should try all, or at least most, of the below methods before we ask the developer ourselves.

The reason we should try ourselves is twofold, first because, as mentioned above, it can often be more efficient and take less time for us to get our answer. Second, it builds our independence and our own skills, making us less dependent on other people in the future.

Search the support forum

From my own observations, over 40% of questions that I see on support forums, have been asked before. If I am responding with an answer I simply find a link to that thread and post it, or I cut and paste the answer.

Failing to do even a basic search before submitting our support request simply wastes everyone's time and often, especially if it is a common question, the only answer we will get is a curt "search the forum that has already been asked before".

If we search the forum, then we can often cut out several hours, or even days, of wait time and get our answer now. At the very least, if our search returns nothing then we can be confident that it's a new problem and worth bringing up.

When searching, we should try to be creative with our search strings:

- If there is an error message, put all or part of it in the post. The same goes for error codes.
- Try shorter strings before longer ones.
- Try different ways of wording the problem "will not delete", "can't remove", "cannot get rid of", and so on as people express things differently.

 If we did search the forum but failed to find anything, then saying so in our support request will win you some goodwill with the developers because we showed some initiative instead of just expecting them to solve everything for us.

Search the Internet

As with searching the forum, searching the Internet can often give us our answer without needing to wait for it. For very popular extensions, PHP or JavaScript errors, or the Joomla! core itself this should probably be the first place we try, even before the developer's site.

 Just like forum searching, mentioning that we have already searched the Internet can boost our chances of a positive support response.

Read the Manual/FAQ

Not all Joomla! extensions come with manuals, but if the one we are working on has a manual or FAQ page then we should probably check it out after we do our searches, but before we make a support request. Often, common problems are listed on these pages.

Ask a skilled friend

This option may not be available to all of us, but if we have a friend or associate who is a Joomla! expert, then they might have experienced the problem we are facing. We must be careful not to abuse this assistance however, as they may not want to remain our friend for long if all they spend their time doing is helping us on our site. We need to remember to be considerate of their time.

Support requests

If all of the above fail, it's time to head to the developer and submit a support request of some kind.

There are several different methods we can use for submitting our request, each with their own strengths and benefits. Which ones are available to us depends on the extension developer.

Forums

If available, a forum should be our first choice when submitting support requests. This is for one main reason, many more eyes on a single problem. Often, a question posted on a public forum won't be answered by the staff, but by other community members and customers.

Forums are also searchable, so if another person later has the same problem as us they can find our post and see the answer we received, fixing their problem faster than if they had to wait for an answer.

This search ability is also useful for us before we commit to using or purchasing an extension, as we can take a look to see how reliable the support is and how many bugs are in the software.

The downside to forums is that they aren't private, so we need to be careful posting information up there like passwords, our domain, or personal information. Also, in a large, busy forum there is a possibility that our request will get overlooked, especially if it is a poorly written one (as we will discuss next).

Tickets

Tickets are usually the most reliable location for support requests, and are rarely overlooked. They are also usually private, so we can post sensitive information without much fear.

Tickets are useful in that they usually record a history of the issue, allowing us to track what happened and when.

This privacy however makes it difficult, or even impossible, to benefit from previous people's solutions. Often, we will find that if we ask a common question, then we will only get an impersonal, pre-written reply.

Tickets also make it difficult to gauge how widespread problems are with the software before using it, and how responsive the developer is to supporting it.

Email

Email seems to be the preferred method of support for many people. It feels personal to contact someone directly, and makes us comfortable to think that someone we *know* is on the job. But the reality is very different.

Many developers, just like the rest of us, get dozens of emails a day or more. Many of them much more urgent to the developer than our problem. Plus, when reading their email, a developer is often not directly working at that time so will put our request on hold until the next time they are working. As a result, they will occasionally just be forgotten, buried under all the other mails.

On the other hand, a developer will usually only look at the other non-email support avenues when they are actively working and looking for support issues to solve, so the chances of them answering our request promptly are greatly improved.

As we can see, email is potentially the least reliable and timely of the support avenues. To make matters worse, many developers will see it as an invasion of their privacy to be constantly bombarded with "help me" and "fix this" emails in their personal accounts, on their personal time. This makes them reluctant to give us help, and they may just ignore our email altogether.

It is not all bad news however, as email support can be useful and prompt if used in conjunction with a specific, monitored, business only email address.

Support request etiquette

Now that we know the different routes for getting our support, it is time to look at how we can influence the results we get from our requests.

Going to a developer for support is an experience that can be either helpful or painful, depending on two main factors: firstly, the developer's attitude, and secondly our own attitude.

The first one we unfortunately can't do anything about. If a developer doesn't care about supporting their product, there probably isn't anything we can do to change their mind. We have a few alternative options though:

- Hire a skilled developer familiar with the extension to fix it
- Try again to fix it ourselves
- Replace the extension with a different, similar one, or drop the feature altogether

They may not be fantastic options, but they are options.

If the developer is interested in supporting their product however, as it is usually the case, then it is our own attitude and actions that will affect how good the service we receive is.

There are a lot of factors in our behavior that will influence how much and how in depth the support we receive is. Let's take a look at some of these factors and how we can best utilize them to improve our chances of getting good support.

These factors can apply to any of the support routes, forums, tickets, or emails.

Act like we respect the helper and their time

This is the single most important factor in support, and in fact almost every other factor is simply a different way of showing this. If we go into any support request appearing to have no respect or concern for the person on the other end, then the best we can expect is a cold, bare minimum response. At worst, we will get no response now, and possibly none in the future regardless of what we do or say after.

The biggest way to show our respect for other people's time is to put in some effort to make it easier for them to help us out and not just expect them to drop everything they want to do and instead do everything we want them to do.

This is especially important for free extensions, or the Joomla! core itself, because the people answering are working on a totally voluntary basis and are under no obligation to help us. However, it still applies to commercial extensions, because even though we have paid for something we want to receive good service, not just minimum service.

It is also important to show some politeness and personal respect. "Please" and "Thanks" go a long way ensuring prompt, reliable support. Remember that the support person is just as much a human being as we are and we should follow the golden rule of treating them as we would like to be treated.

Choose our forum/category/email target carefully

The people who monitor forums, tickets, and email addresses often are specialized in that area, and may not be in others. In the case of forums, the people viewing that particular forum are interested in that subject.

Posting to the wrong place will make us look like we haven't done any research, or for that matter, care about the protocols of the group. If we don't care about them, why would they want to care about us?

Different mistakes people often make in this factor are:

- Posting a request to the first email address/forum/category that we come across
- Posting to a personal email address of somebody who is neither an acquaintance nor responsible for solving our problem
- Posting a request where it's clearly off topic (such as installation questions in a customizing forum)
- Posting an unrelated question in a thread or ticket that was started with a different problem
- Posting multiple times in different places (this one will get us ignored almost immediately)

Write a useful, meaningful subject line

The subject of our request is one of its most important parts. This is because people scanning tickets, forums, and emails can often identify what it is we want, and if they are able to help us before even looking at our request in detail. It will allow qualified people to find us quickly and unqualified people to not waste their time.

Remember that we want to encourage people to help us, and wasting their time makes them less likely to do so.

Our subject line is not only a description of our problem, but it is also a perfect illustration of ourselves and how much effort we are putting into solving our own problem. People will look at it and can guess immediately what kind of person we are, a needy person who wants a solution done for them, or someone willing to fix the problem themselves who is just looking for a pointer on how to. Only one of these types of people get good support, and I don't think I need to point out which one.

Some common subject lines we can see on forums, and why they are productive or counterproductive, are listed below.

Please help/I need help/can someone help me/help me!!!!!!!!!!

This sort of subject will get ignored as a reflex by almost everyone on a public forum. Paid or dedicated support people will probably read it, but will have a negative attitude about it because they aren't sure if it's for them or another support person.

Because we didn't put any thought or effort into writing a good subject line, other people will think that we are lazy and just want someone to solve our problems for us. Rightly so, they won't want to waste their time on us.

The only worse thing than this is if the title is in all capitals, which is the written equivalent of shouting. All capitals will turn off everyone before they even look at our post.

Urgent/help now/important

Just as bad as the previous subjects, this will turn most people off immediately. The reason being that our deadline simply isn't as important as their own deadlines.

A subject like this is the same as saying to everyone who reads it that our problem is more important than theirs and we think they should stop what they are doing and help us now. This sort of statement is very unlikely to be received well.

Titles like this are actually more likely to get us a slow response or no response at all, so they are totally counterproductive.

Again, all capitals is even worse.

Slideshow module doesn't work

Significantly better than the examples above, this subject may actually attract a couple of passersbys, and will get the right support people helping us out. But it still won't be enthusiastic help.

This sort of subject shows we are prepared to articulate the absolute basics of our problem, but we haven't done any in depth though about it and probably haven't provided much information in our post body.

It also shows we have very little technical knowledge and don't understand what the cause of our problem is, and don't want to find out. Experts want to avoid this kind of support request because they will have to explain everything in great detail to such a person, or have to do the work themselves.

Magic Slideshow V1.02—no animations due to JavaScript error

This is a much, much better subject line. We have the full name of our extension, including the version and we have a clear but concise statement of the problem and cause.

A subject line like this in a public forum is likely to get at least twice as many people read it as the previous subject, and at least ten to twenty times as many as the "Help me" or "Urgent" style subject. It is also much more likely to attract someone who has actual experience with our problem and is willing to help us.

It tells people that we know what we are talking about and that we have personally investigated and understood our problem but can't fix it, rather than just running here at the first sign of trouble.

Provide as much information as possible

When writing the body of our support request, it is very important that we provide as much information as possible. This is so that the people providing us with support can give us more accurate responses, and are inclined to give them.

This also saves a lot of time because if we don't provide any information, then the first thing we will be asked is to provide some basic information before they begin to diagnose our problem. No matter what happens, we need to provide this information at some point, so if we provide it up front we will get a faster response, and a more enthusiastic one.

For example, we wouldn't walk into a doctor's office and say, "Doc, I am sick, make me better," and expect them to know exactly what is wrong and what to do about it would we? Well we shouldn't do the same to support people because they can't help us without information.

Some points to explain when writing our body:

- The environment on our server
- The browsers where the problem occurs (if a front end issue)
- The version of Joomla! we are running
- The version of the extension(s) in question
- The URL of our site, preferably a link to the problem page
- Any error messages that are output
- Any research or testing you did and the results of that testing/research
- A screenshot of the problem if possible
- A detailed description of the symptoms and how to replicate it

The sort of request below, for example, will probably get us no response at all, or simply a question asking for more information and a link to the page.

The slideshow has a bug and doesn't work.

Can someone fix it for me?

This sort of request is unproductive for a few reasons. First, we have publicly insulted the developers and their skills by assuming there is a bug in their code when it could be something we have done wrong. There are likely to be many other users who aren't experiencing our problem. We shouldn't cry "bug" unless we have, or can provide a copy of, the problem code to back our claims up; otherwise this is likely to make the developers unhappy with us, even if it is actually a bug.

Second, there is no information at all to give the support people any idea what our problem actually is. As a result, this sort of question will take at least twice as long for us to get an answer to, than if we wrote our question well.

Third, we have come across as someone who doesn't want to fix their problem, but someone who wants their problem fixed. Skilled developers are often eager to give advice to people who want to fix their problems, but try to avoid people who want their problems fixed. This is because the latter types of people usually require a lot of work to assist, but the former usually just need to be pointed in the right direction.

A better request would be like the one below.

> *I have installed version 1.02 of the Magic slideshow into Joomla 1.5.10 but when I view a page with it loaded in Internet Explorer 6 or 7 it doesn't move.*
>
> *I found that it worked if I changed the template. Does anyone have any ideas how I can try to work out the problem?*
>
> *The problem page is http://www.blahblah.com, you can see the slideshow at the top of the page under the menu.*

Here we have provided all the information needed to make a basic diagnosis, and the developers can even check out our site to see it for themselves without having to ask us to for a link and then wait for us to post it.

It also shows that we have put some time into trying to diagnose the problem ourselves, and that we are prepared to fix it ourselves if we get the right information.

Taking the an extra minute or two when writing our support request and putting in some extra information will almost always take hours or even days off the time it takes to solve our problem, so there is absolutely no excuse not to do it.

Summary

We should now be much better equipped to tackle problems with our site.

We looked at how we can diagnose and fix some common problems with Joomla! sites.

We also now understand the implications and risks of customizing our site, and using extensions that hack the Joomla! core.

Finally, we talked about the best practices when going to others for assistance and support, and the how to go about it so that we get the most positive and helpful responses we can.

10
Promoting and Tracking

Having our site ready to go is not much use to us unless we can get people to visit it. Furthermore, it's difficult to tell how many people we are attracting, and if they are joining us or not, without some way of tracking their visits and progress through our site.

To help with these important tasks, we will spend this chapter going over how we can promote and track our site and make use of some great Joomla! resources while doing so. Specifically, we will look at:

- Promoting our site
- Traditional marketing methods
- Social media marketing methods
- Tracking visitors to our site

Promoting our site

Promotion of our site is one of the most vital parts, and yet sadly, one of the aspects many web site owners pay the least attention to. Without solid promotion, our site, no matter how good, is unlikely to ever see any great success.

I think of site promotion as being roughly broken into three aspects, Search Engine Optimization (SEO), traditional marketing techniques, and social media based promotion.

SEO

SEO is the process of designing or adjusting our site to improve its rankings in search engine results. This is usually done to improve the volume and quality of visitors to our site from organic search engines such as Google, Yahoo, or Live MSN.

The most commonly known aspect of the influence of SEO is the Google Page Rank. It is a number from 0 to 10, indicating how important Google believes a certain page to be.

There are a lot of things we can do to improve the SEO of our site.

Web page URLs

Being a content management system, Joomla! works by storing the information we want to display in a database and then loading it into the page according to the destination URL. This will often result in a web page URL that looks something like:

```
http://www.mysite.com/index.php?option=com_content&view=article&id
=19&Itemid=27
```

Several years ago, this URL wouldn't have been indexed at all by most of the major search engines because of the question mark and ampersands in it. Replacing our database URLs with plain text ones was vital to getting on a search engine at all, let alone achieving a high ranking.

Luckily that has changed. All of the major search engines can now traverse database-powered sites like Joomla! sites properly.

Technically speaking, there is no pressing SEO need to do something about our URLs, but there can be some benefits as some search engines place importance on keywords that are present in the URL. Also, from a usability point of view, it is much easier for our visitors to remember links to our pages when we give them something readable. The following URL, for example, is much more user friendly than our original, even though they may point to the same page.

```
http://www.mysite.com/why-seo-matters.html
```

We have already installed the component SH404 SEF into our site in an earlier chapter, so there is no need for us to do anything else now. It was worth bringing it up again however, because of the link to SEO.

Content

One of the most important aspects of SEO is the content on our site and how well it relates to the type of customers we are trying to attract.

There will always be certain keywords that are likely to be searched for by the visitors we are trying to attract. For example, on our sample site, we are trying to attract people interested in having a house in Japan. These people are likely to search for keywords like 'house in japan', 'live in japan', and so on.

With these keywords in mind, we should use them in our content whenever appropriate, and in turn favor them over terms less likely to be searched for such as 'get a place in japan'.

We need to make sure that we are using the keywords appropriately in our content, because while it might be tempting to write articles that are simply stuffed with keywords and contain little or no real information, in an attempt to fool search engines into giving our site a better position, search engines are actively on the lookout for such sites. When we are caught, we may be removed from the search engine listings altogether, so it is not worth the risk.

Besides keywords, filling our site with good, useful content will also bring us more backlinks as people recommend our articles to others. So while keyword placement should always be kept in consideration, consistent, high quality content will bring many more benefits to our site in the longer term than keyword stuffing our pages.

Metadata

As mentioned in an earlier chapter, it is important for us to have relevant metadata for as many pages as possible on our site. This is particularly important for our content pages.

Metadata for our content can be found in the **Article Edit** screen, on the right-hand side under the **Metadata Information** heading. We may need to click the heading to open the panel.

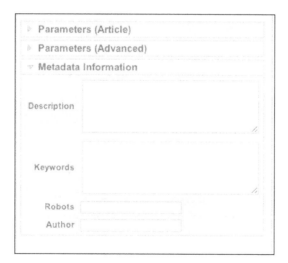

The metadata consists of four fields, but only three of them concern us right now.

The **Description** section should contain a brief summary of the page, preferably with a few keywords in it. Try to keep this description under 200 characters as most search engines won't read more than that.

The **Keywords** section is for us to specifically stuff in keywords that are relevant to the page, separated by commas. Again try to keep this to under 200 characters for the same reason as the description above.

We should try to have the description, keywords, and our content share similar keywords. It's no use writing about the eating habits of Siberian tigers, only to put in metadata keywords of 'New York' and 'Ferrari'.

Finally, the **Author** section is for us to optionally put the author's name if we feel it will help the SEO of the page.

For Joomla!, there are several useful extensions we can use to help us in this department.

The first is the **Missing Metadata** module, from `http://www.joomlajumpstart.com`. This module goes into our administrator panel and lists any content items that have missing metadata.

Another is **Tag Meta**, from `http://www.sistemistica.it`. This extension gives us finer control over some of the metadata that appears on our site.

Images on our site

An often-overlooked aspect of SEO is images on a site. Images can help in two ways, boosting the SEO of the page itself, but also by appearing in image search results such as on Google and Yahoo. For some keywords, it is much easier to get an image on the first page of image searches than a site on the first page of site searches.

Obviously appearing in Google image search won't help every site, but it can help many.

Some tips for images are listed in the following sections.

Image alt text

This should contain a short description of the image as if we were explaining it to someone who couldn't see it. If possible try to squeeze in a keyword or two. For example:

A young man standing in front of his traditional Japanese style House.

Title text

This should contain the information we want people to see when moving their mouse over the image. While our `alt` text, that we mentioned above, should be a description of the image appearance, the `title` should be more a description of its function or purpose.

Continuing our example from above, we might have a title of:

Me in Japan standing in front of my new house.

As we can see, we have squeezed in a couple of keywords, while still keeping the text legitimate and useful to real people.

Text surrounding the image

Most search engines realize that it's difficult to capture the full meaning of a picture into the `alt` and `title` attributes. Instead, they use the text near the image to get a better idea of its purpose. Because of this, we should be careful where we position our images and place them near text that is most relevant to the image.

File name

The file name will also be read when indexing an image, so names like `img1234.jpg` are virtually useless, whereas our image we mentioned above could be named something like `my-japanese-house-and-i.jpg`, giving it a name that is both useful and keyword rich.

Inbound links

While not directly under the umbrella of SEO, **inbound links**, also called **backlinks** are one of the most crucial ingredients to moving up the search results ladder. The more links we have from other sites to ours, the more relevant our site will appear to search engines. After all, if people are linking to us then we must have useful content, and if we have useful content then people will want to read it more than a site that doesn't have popular content.

Inbound links can be gained via link trades, but the best way is simply to have good content and encourage visitors to share it.

Outbound links

When Google analyses a page, it checks all of the links going out of that page, and considers each link a 'vote' for the page it links to. It then divides the page rank of the original page into as many pieces as there are links, and weighs the votes of those links accordingly.

As a result, each link of a page rank 8 site that has 500 external links may, in fact, carry less weight than the single link on a page rank 5 site that only has that one external link.

We can use this methodology to our advantage via the link attribute `rel="nofollow"`. This attribute tells search engines not to pass any page rank to that site. To use this attribute, just put it in the html tag for the link as shown below.

```
<a href="http://www.mysite.com" rel="nofollow">Go there!</a>
```

We can use this, for example, on any links that go off of our site to other sites with which we don't have some sort of relationship, and not apply it to links that are internal to our site, to sites we own, or to partner sites, subtlety boosting the page rank of those sites.

SEO consists of a lot more than just this, and the tactics employed shift regularly as search engines refine their algorithms, as other companies bring out new ideas or systems, and unfortunately as spammers and black hat SEO operators reduce the usefulness of the system.

To keep up on the latest trends, or to get excellent Joomla!-specific SEO advice, I recommend two sites, `http://www.alledia.com` and `http://www. goodwebpractices.com/`. Both are experts in the Joomla! SEO field.

Traditional marketing

The following promotion methods lie in the category of traditional marketing because they are generally the transfer of offline marketing methods into the online environment. As a result, they should be relatively familiar to people.

Advertisements

One of the most common, and for some the most reliable, methods is that of paid advertising. Many people prefer paid advertising over organic visitors, as advertising is more easily adjusted and controlled than search results are.

Many people choose to market solely through Google Adwords (`adwords.google. com`) who are, to my knowledge, still the biggest advertiser around today.

One of the great things about Adwords is that it allows us to run multiple advertisements at the same time and track the click through rates on each one.

This way we can see which of our ads is generating a stronger response, and then remove the non-performing ones, and then try some new variations on the wording of the successful ones.

As an alternative to Google Adwords, there are many other advertising companies, and many sites manage their own advertising internally. Often, the best way to get advertising on a site that would be useful to us, such as being in a similar niche, is to contact the administrators of a site, or look around the site for a page with advertising information.

Mailing list

Another popular marketing technique is using **mailing lists**. We collect email addresses and names from people interested in hearing from our site and then we regularly send them more information.

A mailing list is slightly different from the other techniques because it is focused more on getting customers to return and continue their relationship with our site than to bring people to our site that have never visited before.

Getting people to sign up for a mailing list can be done in several ways, the least effective of which is simply to put a form up on the site and ask people to sign up.

Most effective email marketers use a more productive method, which is to offer people something valuable as a reward for signing up for the list such as a free report, video, or ebook.

With a mailing list, the most important point is to provide useful interesting material to our readers and not just repetitive marketing and sales pitches. If we do the latter, then we will just drive people to unsubscribe without ever giving us a chance. On the other hand, if we spend our energy on giving to our readers instead, then we stand a much better chance of succeeding.

It is also important to decide if we will host our mailing list on our own server, or on a dedicated email hosting service. I usually recommend getting a dedicated service, because if we are sending mail from our own servers, using our own email addresses, and (heaven forbid) a large number of readers flag our emails as spam, we could find our domain on an email spammer list.

If we are put onto such a list at a large mail provider such as Gmail, Yahoo, or Hotmail, we could find that the bulk of our emails are blocked before they even reach reader's inboxes, including all emails and not just our mailing list! Large mailing list providers however, usually have agreements in place with the large email providers to not block mail coming from them. Thus, improving our chances of reaching our customers.

Article marketing

Article marketing is where a company produces one or more short articles on topics related to their industry and then have these articles published on dedicated article submission sites, but sometimes they could be published on partner's sites, tutorial sites, or even in online magazines.

These articles will almost always have a section after, or before, the article detailing the author with a link to their web site.

Article marketing can be very effective because the article submission directories often rank quite highly in search engines. This can help us in two ways.

First, it helps by providing a quick way to jump up the search engine rankings, as the article will have a higher chance of moving up the rankings than a brand new site. Then people reading our article will hopefully choose to visit our site as well.

Second, it helps our site by providing authoritive links back to our site from a well-ranked page. This will, over time, increase the importance of our site in the eyes of the search engines.

The articles will usually not be about our site itself, but rather about something that is related to our site. In our case, we might submit articles on buying property in Japan or how to deal with mortgage banks in Japan.

An added bonus is that industry magazines or big sites will sometimes pick up articles from these sites, republishing them on their own sites along with credit to us and a link to our site. As a result, we will usually get a spike in traffic during those periods.

Article submission sites can be easily found using our favorite search engine.

Press release marketing

Very similar to article marketing, **press release marketing** is when we produce press releases about our site and then submit them to different press release sites.

The main difference here is that the press releases are directly about our company and what we are doing, as opposed to being about a topic relevant to our industry in general like article marketing articles are.

An advantage to press releases are that we can include several links, and more direct links to our site, whereas normal articles are limited to the author biography section only.

As with article marketing, many press release submission sites can be found via our favorite search engine, but it is important to pick our press release sites more carefully than we would with article submission sites. This is because press releases are directly associated with our web site and business.

If the site we post them to is full of blatantly keyword stuffed releases with no real information, or cheap sales pitches over and over, then people will begin to associate our site with these sorts of sites. This will be potentially damaging to our reputation. Instead, we want to be selective to post our releases on sites that are involved with our business niche and seem to have press releases of real value on them.

Social marketing

Where traditional marketing is generally one way marketing, with us sending information to prospective customers in order to get them to our site, social marketing is more oriented around give and take. Communicating with our prospects rather than providing direct sales pitches to them.

With successful social marketing, we will rarely, if ever, make direct sales pitches to our prospects. The aim is to provide enough value to them that they naturally come to us for more.

Blogging

Most people are familiar with blogging by now. It is basically the process of having an online journal where we write our thoughts, ideas, discoveries, or what we are doing. Usually blog posts are several hundred words in length and include images as well as links to other sites.

A blog that is nothing but sales pitch after sales pitch, or is just plain boring, is not going to be effective because no one will want to read it. A successful blog, however, provides regular, useful information that people want to hear about, and want to continue to hear about.

Blogging allows our prospects to see the human side of us, and fosters a feeling of knowing us. This is especially true if we have comments or discussion areas and participate in them with our readers.

Once we have built a level of trust with our readers, they will often naturally want to learn more about us. If they have a need for the type of products and services we provide, then it is more likely that they will go with someone they know and trust (us) than someone they don't.

Social networking sites

There are a number of big social networking sites around today, and more arriving every day. Each with different abilities and a different aim for their site. We can make use of some of these sites, such as those listed below, to help with our business.

Twitter (www.twitter.com)

Twitter is the current leader in a trend known as micro-blogging. Where instead of being several hundred words long, posts, or tweets as they are called, are kept at 140 characters or less. This allows for a single medium to long sentence or two to three short sentences.

Twitter is a great way to communicate with potential customers, and commonly it is used to have short conversations, pass useful information, or offer assistance to people who might need it.

Twitter accounts are really only useful to a business if they have a steady stream of followers. A useful way to build up our followers is to find people who are interested in the same things we are, and then follow them. In many cases, we will get a return follow.

How do we find people with similar interests? The easiest way is to use the twitter search functionality that will search for what are called **hashtags**. Hash tags are use by people making a tweet to identify the key subject or subjects in a tweet. They are indicated by putting a hash mark in front of the keyword. For example, a tweet that might indicate someone of interest to our sample site could be along the lines of:

I am looking forward to moving to #Japan next year.

We can also use hashtags in our own posts to help attract other people who might be searching on twitter. Using this method, we should try to inject at least one, and no more than three, relevant hashtags into a large number of our tweets. If a particular post doesn't have any hashtag worthy words in it, then it's better not to try and force one in because again, it will become obvious to people that we are trying to game the system.

There are also a lot of automated services around for Twitter, many designed specifically to assist people with marketing their products or service. Some of these are useful and others not so useful.

Some that are useful are services that aggregate or do deeper searches on twitter, allowing us to find people talking about us, our products or related areas, even if not hashtagged.

Some to avoid are services that do automatic posting. People who have automated twitter streams are very easy to spot and quickly lose any quality followers due to the lack of variety and endless spam of their tweets. I experienced someone doing this myself when they posted that were off to bed, then continued to post almost every 20 seconds for the next 8 hours. When I check my tweet list an hour later over 70% of the tweets listed were from this person with special offers, links to great deals, and one time only opportunities. Needless to say, I unfollowed them soon after.

Another useful concept for us is the idea of "re-tweeting" or taking someone else's tweet, marking it with their name, and forwarding it on. By re-tweeting any relevant, or interesting, tweets from our customers, or potential customers, we can get their attention as well as show that we pay attention to them and are interested in sharing and not in simply selling to people.

It can also work in our favor if we make re-tweet worthy tweets, because as our followers re-tweet them, other people will be exposed to us at no cost to ourselves.

We need to remember that in order for it to work, social media must be a two way communication, and not one way as with traditional marketing.

Facebook (www.facebook.com)

Facebook is more fully featured than Twitter, and allows people to host photos, have real conversations, live chat, install, and use custom applications and games and much more. It also allows us to create a full profile of ourselves and our organization, which people can view and interact with.

Facebook is still similar to Twitter in respect that it encourages us to regularly interact with our friends and associates. It provides many different avenues for doing so, be it commenting on photos, chatting, playing games, or other activities.

For our site, we can use Facebook both as a source of incoming links, but also as a general way to get information out to many of our prospects who might be frequent Facebook users. We should set up our account with a lot of information about our site, products and services, including images, text, and links.

LinkedIn (www.linkedin.com)

Where Facebook is more social acquaintance-focused, **LinkedIn** is a social networking site focused more on building and growing business relationships.

Depending on our site's needs, we are very likely to be able to find and build business-to-business relationships, or find professional prospects on this site.

LinkedIn has less social activities and applications available than Facebook, but instead has a focus on posting resumes and company information.

LinkedIn is potentially much more useful for a site that is developed around a single person and their services, as their credentials can become an advertisement.

MySpace (www.myspace.com)

Some people view **MySpace** as a "Facebook for kids". This is reflected in the much younger average user age of MySpace. As a result of this, it is often easy for a web site to decide where to focus their social efforts by looking at the type of customers they are trying attract.

For example, a business that was based around music and fashion might find a better reception on MySpace than one based on home ownership like our sample site.

In all of the above cases, once we have an account at a social media site we should put an appropriate, and prominent, link to it on our main site, so that people who visit our site can also communicate with us via the social media site of their choice.

Tagging and Social Bookmarking sites

Social Bookmarking is the process of Internet users using specialized sites to store, organize, and manage lists of web site bookmarks, and also to often associate metadata to these links in the form of tags.

The main purpose behind storing these bookmarks on a web site rather than on our own computer is for the purpose of sharing them with others. It is this sharing we want to encourage from our users.

The easiest way to encourage bookmarking and sharing among our users is by providing them with buttons allowing them to bookmark our pages with a single click.

There are a lot of Joomla! extensions that will allow us to put these buttons on our sites, and they can be found in the **Communities & Groupware | Social Bookmarking** category in the Joomla! Extensions directory: `http://extensions.joomla.org/extensions/communities-&-groupware/social-bookmarking`.

Most of these simply require us to install and publish a plugin or module to get the benefits of these extensions. When placing buttons like these on our sites, we should keep in mind that certain social networking are general and others are focused on specific niches. Chose to put links to only those sites that are relevant to our own.

Forums and comments

Forum and content marketing does not relate to using our own forums and comments, but rather to participating in the forums and offering comments on popular sites related to our site's niche market.

Then we place a link back to our web site into the signature of our account. This provides us with linkbacks and advertising every time we post.

It is important that when doing forum and comment marketing that we actually make useful posts and contribute to the conversation. Making pointless posts simply to get more links will be obvious. Not only will people lose respect for our brand and site, but we may end up being banned from the site in question for being spammers.

By contributing actively and becoming an important part of other communities, we can also build a personal reputation as being an authority in a particular area. Becoming an authority will increase our reputation and bring even more people to our site.

Even if a forum doesn't allow live links in a signature block, having our web site URL in there as flat text can still bring people who copy the link into their browsers.

Tracking visitors to our site

It is important for us to be able to track and monitor visitors to our site. This is so we can see which of our advertising campaigns, partner sites, or search keywords is bringing us the most traffic.

There are many good analytics applications available such as:

- Google Analytics (`http://www.google.com/analytics/`)
- Piwik (`http://piwik.org/`)
- Mint (`http://haveamint.com/`)
- Woopra (`http://www.woopra.com/`)
- Clicky (`http://getclicky.com/`)
- crazyegg (`http://crazyegg.com/`)

Each of these has different benefits and features. Some of them are free and others are a paid service.

Many people's first experience with web analytics is with Google Analytics. This is because it is free and hosted, so there is nothing needed except to get an account and add some JavaScript to our site. Let's take a look at Google Analytics and how we can use it with our site.

Google Analytics

The first thing we need to do is visit the Google Analytics homepage. It can be found at: `http://www.google.com/analytics/`.

Once we are there, the next thing to do is create a new account. If we already have a Google account, such as a Gmail account, then we can log into Google Analytics using those credentials. We can sign up for an account by clicking the **Sign Up Now** button to the left of the sign in box.

Once we have signed up and logged in, we will be presented with a screen where we will need to enter some information about the web site we want to track. Information such as: the website's URL, a name for the account it will be organized under (we can add multiple sites to one account if we like), the country, and time zone.

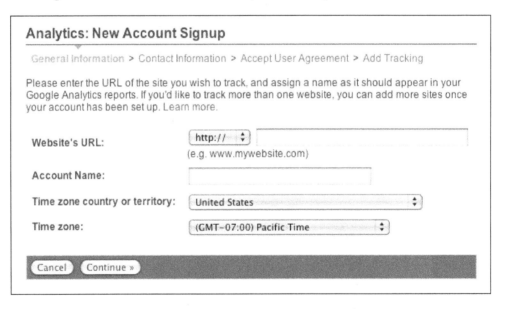

Next, we need to provide some contact information and then accept a user agreement.

The final step is to add some specialized JavaScript to our site that will allow Google Analytics to collect information on people as they navigate our site.

The best place to enter this information is into our template, right before the `</body>` tag at the bottom of the page.

To edit the template, we can open up the `index.php` file on our computer and then FTP it up to the server, or just edit it directly on the server.

To edit it directly on the server, we need to log into our Joomla! site and then go to **Extensions | Template Manager**. Once we are in the **Template Manager**, we need to click on the name of our template to edit it.

Once in the **Template:[Edit]** screen, we then click the **Edit HTML** button in the top-right hand corner.

In the **Template HTML Editor**, we will scroll right to the very bottom where the last few lines should be something like the lines below, which are taken from our same site.

```php
<?php if ($this->countModules('debug')) : ?>
<div class="wrapper"><div class="debug-mod">
    <jdoc:include type="modules" name="debug" style="xhtml" />
</div></div>
<?php endif; ?>
</body>
</html>
```

We want to put the Google Analytics JavaScript code above that `</body>` tag, but after everything else in the template, which will leave us with something like:

```php
<?php if ($this->countModules('debug')) : ?>
<div class="wrapper"><div class="debug-mod">
    <jdoc:include type="modules" name="debug" style="xhtml" />
</div></div>
<?php endif; ?>

<script type="text/javascript">
var gaJsHost = (("https:" == document.location.protocol) ?
  "https://ssl." : "http://www.");
document.write(unescape("%3Cscript src='" + gaJsHost + "google-
analytics.com/ga.js' type='text/javascript'%3E%3C/script%3E"));
</script>
<script type="text/javascript">
try {
var pageTracker = _gat._getTracker("UA-9999999-1");
pageTracker._trackPageview();
} catch(err) {}</script>

</body>
</html>
```

Once we have this code in place, we can save the template. We just need to wait 24 hours for our first day worth of visitors to be collected.

Tracking visitors

Once we have our JavaScript inserted, and have waited 24 hours for data to be collected, we can start to review our site's statistics and use these to make more informed decisions about our site.

First, we will need to log into Google Analytics again and in the center of the page, in the **Website Profiles** section, click the **View report** link to the right of our site name.

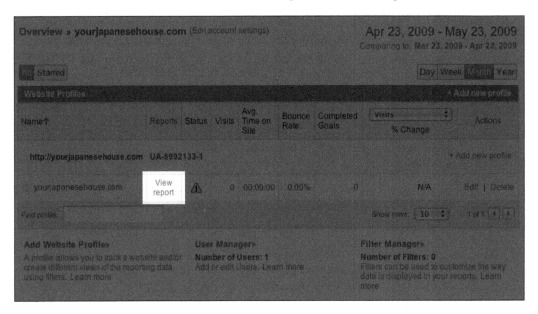

This will open up the **Dashboard** page. At the very top of this page is a chart showing our site traffic for the past month. This allows us to see at a glance if our traffic is growing or shrinking. Because we only put our JavaScript code in 24 hours ago, our chart will be pretty boring. Below is an image of the dashboard for another site that has been tracking for a while.

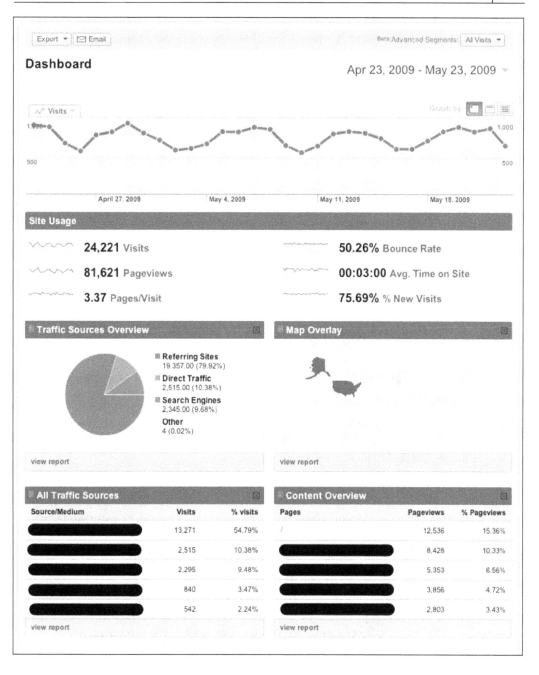

If we want to change the time frame that the chart covers, then we can click on the dates in the upper right-hand corner. We will then see a small calendar display appear, and we can either enter dates manually or click on two dates in the calendar to set them as the boundaries for our new time frame.

To the upper left-hand side of the chart, we will see a small tab with the word **Visits** on it. This indicates what type of data the chart is currently showing. We can change this by clicking on it to let us view the different data. The different options are fairly easy to understand:

- Visits: How many people have visited our site?
- Pageviews: How many times the pages on our site have been viewed?
- Pages/Visit: How many pages users visited on average?
- Avg. Time on Site: How long each user spent on our site?
- Bounce Rate: What percentage of people left after visiting only one page?
- % New Visits: How many of our visitors had never visited our site before?

Immediately below this main chart, we will see a smaller group charts labeled **Site Usage**. Site Usage is merely a quick summary of the available option for the larger graph.

Below **Site Usage**, we have four other charts, each of which gives us summaries of other important information regarding our visitors.

The **Visitors Overview** graph is essentially a summary of the charts above, and while it may seem simply a repeat, the link at the bottom of the chart will allow us to get more detailed information on our visitors.

Beside that is the **Map Overlay** that displays what countries our visitors are coming from. The more visitors that come from a country, the darker green it will become. This can be useful to us when determining if we should be catering to other languages or nationalities with our content.

The next one is **Traffic Sources Overview**, which shows a pie graph of how our users are finding their way to our site. It shows if our traffic is coming from visitors directly typing in the URL, from search engines, or from other sites sending them to us. Clicking the view report link here will allow us to drill-down into this information much more deeply and see exactly which sites are directing people to us, and which search terms are bringing people to our site.

Finally, we have **Content Overview**, which shows us the top five most viewed pages over the time period we specified above. The view report link here will allow us to see how long our visitors stayed on each page, where they came from, and where they went after viewing the page.

On the left-hand side of the page, we can see the menu illustrated below. Under each of the options on this menu are many more report options for tracking who our visitors are, where they came from, and what they looked at.

The bottom most option, **Goals**, can be used by us to set goals for our site such as getting people to visit a certain page, or sign up. We can then track how successful we are with those goals.

There is lot more to Google Analytics, and as mentioned above. There are many other options for site analytics, some with more features, and some simply with different features. A quick search on the internet will reveal many articles on advanced analytics usage, tips and tricks, and it is well worth getting familiar with an analytics tool.

Summary

We should now understand some of the many ways we can market our site, and thus increase its effectiveness. We should also now understand ways to track our visitors so we can understand more about where they come from, and what they are interested in.

We should understand the three marketing aspects, SEO, social marketing, and traditional marketing, and be able to make informed decisions about which of these will best suit our site and give us the best chances of success.

This knowledge, if used correctly, can mean the difference between a barren site with no visitors or a busy site with many new members and a thriving community growing around it.

11
Monetizing Our Site

The last topic we are going to look at, monetizing our site, is really something that we should keep in mind the whole time that we are planning and developing it. We have mentioned it several times already, but it is worth devoting some time to properly understanding it.

Monetizing is adding features to our site in order to allow us to earn money from it. To help us get a strong understanding of how we can do this we will take a look at the following:

- The Internet and the free economy
- Monetization models
- Monetization methods
- Implementing monetization on our site

The Internet and the free economy

On the Internet today there is a constant push by people to receive more for less, and as a result it is very easy to get a hold of vast quantities of information, media, and entertainment for little or no cost. This has resulted in many, if not most, users assuming the Internet as a big free storehouse of whatever they want.

For a while this economy seemed sustainable as hardware and bandwidth prices dropped dramatically, and investors poured money into different sites during the dot com boom. But many web sites focussed more on getting visitors than building a sustainable business model, which is part of what lead to the subsequent bust.

This difficulty in monetization has persisted through to today, with only a few of the Internet's biggest sites actually turning a profit. The rest, like Facebook, rely mainly on investor's capital to fill the gap, like Facebook, or the support of a profitable mother company such as with Google and YouTube.

What does this have to do with us? Well we are going to produce a site that is both profitable and has some appeal in the free economy. But this requires a bit of thought and planning.

We need to make sure we are turning a profit because otherwise, it's a pointless business. Traditional marketing methods, however, don't work well in a free economy, so we need to be creative.

Monetization models

There are five main models used for monetization on the Internet, the features of which often overlap one another making it sometimes difficult to determine which model is which.

Advertising

Advertising is a favored income stream of many people, particularly bloggers and sites offering an otherwise free service or product.

In this model, our income would come almost entirely from other people who are trying to sell their products and services to our visitors.

Advertising is generally only effective on high traffic sites, because most web users ignore a majority of advertising reflexively. We need to put an advertisement in front of a lot of people before we can find people who will click on them.

There are many approaches that we can take to put advertising on our site.

Google Adwords

One of the most common advertising methods, Google Adwords is a system where semi-random advertisements are placed on our site by Google, who then pays us a small percentage of the income they make selling that advertising space to other people.

Adwords is generally best for lower to medium traffic sites, as private advertisers (see below) are often difficult for these sites to attract. Adwords is also very easy to setup and maintain, as Google handles all the client invoicing, ad selections, content association and so on. So it is very much a fire and forget system.

It is also, however, one of the least profitable advertising approaches, which is the price we pay for it being one of the easiest work with.

Other advertising services

Besides Google Adwords, there are dozens, if not hundreds, of other smaller advertising suppliers. Some of these provide only text-based advertisements, some images and other media only, and some provide both.

These advertising suppliers also vary in the returns they provide. Some are better suited to specific niches. It may be worth looking into alternatives for Google Adwords if after trying Adwords out, we find that it sends us inappropriate advertisements or that we aren't getting very much of a response to the advertisements.

Private advertisers

Best suited for very high traffic sites, privately soliciting and maintaining advertisers is usually the most profitable method of advertising because we are able to set our own prices instead of relying on an advertising supplier to set them for us.

For low traffic sites, private advertising can be useful if our site is in a certain unique niche and related advertisements don't often appear in Adwords or other advertising suppliers.

Private advertising is also the hardest work of all the advertising methods, because it is up to us to invoice and maintain the advertisements correctly.

Affiliate advertising

Affiliate advertising is sometimes closer to selling products and services than to true advertising, but often people use affiliate advertising as a substitute for private advertising.

For example, they will put up a banner for the affiliate program on their site just as they might put up a banner for a private advertiser. Instead of being paid a set fee by the advertiser, they get paid a commission on any sales made to people clicking on their affiliate banner.

Affiliate advertising is the least predictable of the advertising methods, as our income is determined entirely by how well the advertiser is able to sell to people. With standard advertising we only have to get people to go to their site, or in some cases we can charge for simply showing the ad, regardless of how many clicks it receives.

Because of this, affiliate advertising can be either very profitable on the right site, or generate almost no profits if products are chosen poorly.

Selling information

Selling information usually revolves around tutorials on how to do something, and it could be flat text, a PDF file, an HTML page, videos, audio, or anything else that can be used to convey information.

A prominent example is `lynda.com` which sells subscriptions to information videos.

Selling information is usually done in one of two ways, either a one off payment for access to a certain amount of non changing information, such as an eBook or a video set, or alternatively as a subscription model for access to regularly updated information, such as a news site, or an ever expanding video library.

Both models have their merits. The one off payment model will probably generate less revenue over time, as subscriptions are renewable, but it will require a lot less maintenance since once it is operating it will need only to be kept running. On the other hand, the subscription model will require new content to be produced regularly.

Selling products

Selling products is a fairly easy to understand concept as it is essentially the same as in the offline world.

Products could be electronic, such as e-books, music, or computer programs, or they could be real, physical products that need to be shipped to a customer.

Internet-based stores are very convenient because they are open 24 hours a day, and the whole world now becomes a potential customer.

Selling services

A companion to selling products, selling services is another viable route to take to monetize our site.

Similar to products, the services could be electronically delivered, web site hosting, media uploading and storing, chat services and so on, or they could be physical off line services plumbing, medical, transportation, or almost anything else that could be done offline.

Monetization implementations

There is a potentially unlimited number of ways we can implement the above models, and our options are really only limited our imagination. The main point to keep in mind is that we need to provide a certain level of value to people, enough value to make it worth paying for. This value could be a real, measurable value, such as in the case of a physical product or a perceived, emotional value such as higher status in a social network.

There are some common methods of implementation though that are worth looking at. Both of these are very compatible with a free economy, as the primary product is mostly provided for free.

Freemium

A freemium is where a portion of a service or part of an information product is given away for free to entice people to try it out, and then once they are interested in the service/product they are up sold to the complete service.

This is a very common method in use by many web services today because of its effectiveness. A higher percentage of people will often purchase a quality product if they can try it, than would purchase it if they couldn't try it.

This only applies to quality products, however, and low quality products or services may actually find their sales drop by implementing a freemium model.

These are especially effective with electronically delivered goods and services, because the intrinsic costs of maintaining a web site can be very low, so only a tiny percentage of people actually need to sign up in order to support the majority who are using the free service.

It is especially effective for services such as social media sites, where the number of people using it determines the value of the service. Providing many of the features for free builds up the value of the service and makes it easier to sell to people than simply charging for it completely.

Freemium methods often need only rely on a 99%-1% ratio of free to paid members. With the income from that 1% being enough to cover the other 99%.

Cross subsidy

Cross subsidizing is when something desirable is given away for free, on the condition that something else is purchased.

This model is most easily recognized in the mobile phone industry, where handsets are often given away for free in exchange for the money made on monthly fees for the phone. Hosting companies often give away a free domain registration, or security certificates in exchange for your monthly hosting fees.

It could also be implemented as a software program being given away for free, but requiring a monthly subscription to get the best benefits.

Advertising removal

Sometimes taking something away can be just as effective in motivating people as giving them something. In this case, giving people the option to remove advertisements from our site in return for a nominal subscription can be a potential motivator.

This method is more often associated with software, where advertisements or pop-up boxes requesting a donation are included. These can be removed by licensing your version of the software.

Monetization models for our site

We discussed the monetization of our own site briefly when we were deciding on which extensions we wanted to install. We have come to the point now that we want to refine and focus our monetization plan and work out the best way to implement our chosen extensions, and add more if needed.

Initially, we discussed using two main models for our site, advertising and subscriptions. But after some more thought, we are going to add in a further revenue source, that of professional services. This will be an attempt to do some consulting based around the knowledge we will be producing.

It is very helpful to have multiple streams of income from a site, as it makes the income more robust overall. Many sites rely on only a single source of income and if something happens to that source, they could be left with nothing without warning.

Let's now look at these different streams in detail.

Advertising

For our niche, we could definitely make use of both advertising company adverts and private advertising as well. This is because the real estate industry, and related services such as house maintenance, insurance, and so on is very large. It will be possible to get enough relevant results from Google Adwords to make it useful to our visitors, but also competitive enough that some people will be willing to privately negotiate more permanent advertisements on our site.

We may also want to look into some affiliate advertising, if we can find some that will appeal to our visitors.

Google Adwords

One of the benefits for subscribers will be the removal of advertisements for a cleaner, clutter free site. We will, however, only be removing the Google ads, as any private advertising will be handled in a less obtrusive way than the Google ads.

The Google ads will be spread on most pages of our site to get maximum exposure, but will be positioned with the private advertising more prominent. This is because we are aiming to make more from the private advertising than the Google advertising.

The Google advertising is also our least important income stream, and partly here to encourage people to sign up for an ad-free reading experience.

Private advertising

Initially, it will be difficult to get good prices for private advertising until we get our traffic up. But once we have some steady traffic, we should be able to attract some.

Attracting private advertisers can be done passively or actively.

Passively, as the name implies, requires the least amount of effort to put in place. It will usually entail us putting up a few boxes with 'advertise here' on them and a link to a page with details and pricing of advertising placements. Then we sit and wait for people to contact us.

While easy to do, it will usually bring us less advertisers overall and less income per advertiser. This is because many potential advertisers are often too busy with their own site to be surfing to ours. Or they may not even spend time surfing, and use their web site simply as a digital business card. We will only be able to attract advertisers who actually come to our site.

Actively looking for advertisers can be a long process. Many of the people we contact won't be interested in advertising on our site, or can't afford it. This will be especially true when we first start out with our site before we build up traffic. Actively looking, however, gives us more flexibility in our arrangements and we may be able to organize higher prices, or discounts for our members or some other alternative to direct advertising.

We will use a mix of these two for our benefit. For the first six months or so of our site's life, while we build our traffic base, we will operate mainly on passively attracting advertisers. This is because actively looking for them will likely be a waste of time early on without any evidence of traffic to back up our prices.

Also, many potential advertisers will be influenced by how our site ranks in Google, Alexa, and our Google Page Rank. All of these things can take time for us to build up to where they are attractive to advertisers.

Then once we are averaging around 2-500 unique visitors a day, and have a Google Page Rank of at least four, we can start seriously looking for advertisers while being able to ask decent prices.

Depending on our traffic, an amount between $50 and $200 a month is often easy to justify for a small advertisement of around 200 x 200 pixels, with larger advertisements priced more highly.

For us, something else to consider is that our visitors are mainly interested in information on high priced items such as houses, loans, and insurance, so we could potentially push our advertising prices even up to 300-500, as even a single referral could amount to thousands, or even tens of thousands, of dollars profit for companies in our niche.

Affiliate advertising

Affiliate advertising will be a good way for us to fill in our private advertising space while we find some private advertisers. Finding some appropriate affiliate programs will probably be difficult for us as "Housing in Japan" is not exactly a high traffic niche.

We will probably be better off to broaden our net and try to find affiliate links related to living in Japan, such as restaurant guides, foreigner services, and so on. These advertisements probably won't generate us a lot of money, but they will allow us to bring some in while we build up traffic without having to justify our prices, or prove our traffic to them, because affiliate programs pay purely on purchases and not on exposures.

Initially, we will be using affiliate advertising with us coming from a weaker position, as we will be trying to build traffic on our new site. Once we have our site established, we can, in addition to changing to active advertising, move to more active affiliates as well.

Seeking more active affiliates will involve striking up partnerships with groups such as insurance or real estate companies, other related web sites or people offering services that our visitors might want. These partnerships would usually involve us being rewarded with a share of profits made from the people we refer to the partner.

Professional services

Our sample site is based around buying and renting property in Japan. In addition to our other income streams, we could offer also offer our visitors and member services such as relocation assistance, assistance with finding properties, translation or interpretation assistance, and so on. All the things that foreigners may find difficult to deal with in Japan.

As these are the things we will be writing about for our articles, it will require us to build up knowledge on these topics. This knowledge can in turn be applied as services.

For some people, particularly web designers, professional services are their primary income source and their information site is purely to bring them potential customers. For us though, it is likely going to be a secondary income stream. We will just do some occasional freelance work to bring in some extra money.

The reason I don't want this to be a big part of our income right now is because professional services are for a single customer and take a lot of time. Whereas if we write an article or secure a partnership deal, that time spent can earn income for us from multiple people over and over, for the same amount of time spent. Ultimately, we want a self-sustaining business that runs without us, and not a self-employed job that we need to manage personally every day.

Because of this, we won't put a high emphasis on the services when designing our site. No significant advertising for the services, simply a page with prices and activities listed.

 If we do somehow get a large number of people contacting us for services, we can always look into hiring someone else to take care of them for us.

Subscriptions

The mainstay of our income at this point is going to be our subscriptions. We want them as our main provider because they are renewable, and our work generating content will be the same regardless of if we have 5 members or 5000 members. This makes it infinitely expandable without major changes to our model.

Just to recap our plans, we have three types of subscriptions:

- Basic — 6 months, 3,900 Yen
- Home Buyer — 1 Year, 5,900 Yen
- Professional — Lifetime, 14,900 Yen

The main thing to think of with subscriptions is that to get people in, and keep them in, we need to provide them with an ongoing value. Luckily, as mentioned above, this value workload isn't really affected by the number of members we have.

We need to divide our value between high initial value to get people wanting to join, and ongoing value to keep them renewing.

There are lots of benefits we can potentially provide to people to encourage them to join up and stay with our site.

Extra content

The primary benefit for becoming a member of our site is going to be access to extra, better content than what is available for free members.

We will provide the majority of our content for free, but keep the most useful articles for our paying members only. We will, however, have teaser articles identifying the articles which we have available for members.

This will also be our strongest ongoing benefit for people. The responsibility though is that we need to keep producing quality, useful material to make it worthwhile to our members to renew.

Advertising removal

As mentioned above, one of the benefits we will provide is to remove the Google advertising from our site for our paying members. We might also want to consider removing some of the lower paying private advertising, or limit the pages it appears on, for our lifetime members.

We can also use this feature to differentiate between low and high cost private advertising.

For example:

- Google ads and private ads for visitors and non-paying members
- Only private ads for Basic members
- Only expensive private ads for Home Owner members
- Expensive private ads only on 'sponsors' page for lifetime members

This would give growing benefits to higher-level members.

Site benefits

We will also give extra privileges on our site to paying members above and beyond the content viewing.

Privileges for now will be basic but will include:

- Ability to post their own house/apartment details in the member gallery
- Guaranteed staff responses (if requested) to their forum posts
- Access to private member forums

These benefits will also help keep people renewing, as they won't want to lose their benefits once they have gained them.

Status

People love to have a higher status than other people, and it can be a strong factor in encouraging people to upgrade if they can raise their status among their peers.

Status will be displayed initially via a banner under their avatar in the forum, but later we will modify our comments and other components to show a user's status around the site.

As with site benefits, people won't want to go back to just being a nobody, so it will encourage many to renew their memberships.

Discounts on services

One strong incentive to sign up could be to offer a discount off the professional services equal to the member's subscription price. This way, no money is lost by the site. However, by gaining a member we can then try to retain them, which is easier than getting a new one.

This would need to be organized as a required purchase before the service is purchased, and not done as a package or after the service has been purchased provided free. Then they will feel more likely to renew this benefit giving subscription, rather than just letting the "free subscription" lapse when time comes to renew.

Discounts from partners

Deals could be made with partners to provide a discount to paying members as a benefit. This can then be a benefit to both our site and the partner's site.

These discounts will probably not be a good incentive to renew unless we add them at regular intervals, such as a "monthly discount". However, they can serve as a good signup motivator, as the discounts can often pay for their subscription itself.

Summary

Monetization of our site is now well in hand. This, combined with our marketing efforts, our consistent and unique site design, our simple but well-chosen extensions and our customization tweaks to improve our site, should result in us earning some money from our business in a reasonably short time. How much effort we put into planning the monetization will be a large factor however, in deciding for us if we earn a real income from our site or just some pocket money.

We should now understand how to bring our site in line with a free economy while still bringing in enough income to support the site.

We also showed, through the example of our sample site, how flexible the implementation of monetization can be.

Index

[PACKT] PUBLISHING

Thank you for buying
Joomla! 1.5x Customization

Packt Open Source Project Royalties

When we sell a book written on an Open Source project, we pay a royalty directly to that project. Therefore by purchasing Joomla! 1.5x Customization, Packt will have given some of the money received to the Joomla! project.

In the long term, we see ourselves and you—customers and readers of our books—as part of the Open Source ecosystem, providing sustainable revenue for the projects we publish on. Our aim at Packt is to establish publishing royalties as an essential part of the service and support a business model that sustains Open Source.

If you're working with an Open Source project that you would like us to publish on, and subsequently pay royalties to, please get in touch with us.

Writing for Packt

We welcome all inquiries from people who are interested in authoring. Book proposals should be sent to author@packtpub.com. If your book idea is still at an early stage and you would like to discuss it first before writing a formal book proposal, contact us; one of our commissioning editors will get in touch with you.

We're not just looking for published authors; if you have strong technical skills but no writing experience, our experienced editors can help you develop a writing career, or simply get some additional reward for your expertise.

About Packt Publishing

Packt, pronounced 'packed', published its first book "Mastering phpMyAdmin for Effective MySQL Management" in April 2004 and subsequently continued to specialize in publishing highly focused books on specific technologies and solutions.

Our books and publications share the experiences of your fellow IT professionals in adapting and customizing today's systems, applications, and frameworks. Our solution-based books give you the knowledge and power to customize the software and technologies you're using to get the job done. Packt books are more specific and less general than the IT books you have seen in the past. Our unique business model allows us to bring you more focused information, giving you more of what you need to know, and less of what you don't.

Packt is a modern, yet unique publishing company, which focuses on producing quality, cutting-edge books for communities of developers, administrators, and newbies alike. For more information, please visit our website: www.PacktPub.com.

PUBLISHING

Building Websites with Joomla 1.5

ISBN: 978-1-847195-30-2   Paperback: 363 pages

This best selling book has now been updated for the latest Joomla 1.5 release

1. Learn Joomla! 1.5 features
2. Install and customize Joomla! 1.5
3. Configure Joomla! administration
4. Create your own Joomla! templates

Learning Joomla! 1.5 Extension Development

ISBN: 978-1-847196-20-0   Paperback: 284 pages

A practical tutorial for creating your first Joomla! 1.5 extensions with PHP, written and tested against the final release of Joomla! 1.5

1. Program your own Joomla! extensions
2. Master Model-View-Controller design
3. Build configurable site modules to show information on every page
4. Use built-in HTML and JavaScript functions

Please check **www.PacktPub.com** for information on our titles